DIVINE
CONTEXT

A Book of Divine Understanding

Volume 1 Old Testament

ANGELO PRINGLE

CLAY BRIDGES
PRESS

Divine Context: Volume 1 Old Testament: A Book of Divine Understanding!

Copyright © 2023 by Angelo Pringle

Published by Clay Bridges Press in Houston, TX
www.ClayBridgesPress.com

All rights reserved. No part of this publication may be reproduced, stored in a retrieval system, or transmitted in any form by any means, electronic, mechanical, photocopy, recording, or otherwise, without the prior permission of the publisher, except as provided for by USA copyright law.

Scripture quotations are taken from the King James Version (KJV): King James Version, public domain.

ISBN: 978-1-68488-076-8 Paperback
eISBN: 978-1-68488-077-5

Special Sales: Most Clay Bridges titles are available in special quantity discounts. Custom imprinting or excerpting can also be done to fit special needs. Contact Clay Bridges at Info@ClayBridgesPress.com

DEDICATION

This book is written in remembrance of all the men and women throughout history who dedicated their lives to preserving the truth of God's most blessed word.

NOTE

The bold printed words presented within each chapter of this book are direct quotes courtesy of the 1611 revised (authorized) King James translation of the Bible along with the chapter and verses, so that the reader can have the opportunity to search the scriptures and confirm that the words being quoted by the author are the words of the Holy Bible. Also, many paraphrases and references have been used within this book in order to add context. The location of the scriptures relating to those paraphrases and references are also included to help the reader understand that the author is speaking from the perspective of the Holy Bible and not from the perspective of himself.

* * *

The New King James version (NKJV), the New International Version (NIV), the Amplified Version, the Contemporary Version, and many more English translations of the Bible all offer us the opportunity to seek God's will. Nevertheless, in my experience, the (authorized) King James (KJV) translation of the Bible offers each of us the best opportunity to receive near-perfect interpretations concerning the holy scriptures. The old English style of the KJV can become cumbersome as we begin to read the Bible, but if we continue to read and become familiar with the scriptures, the old English style of grammar will become an amazing tune within our spirit. Certain translations satisfy the carnal soul, but for me, the AKJV translation satisfies the heavenly spirit. Rev. 13:16 reveals the impact that differing translations can have on our ability to understand God's will, either spiritually or carnally.

Contents

Preface 1
Introduction 3
1. The Light That God Called Day 7
2. The Six Days Of Creation 27
3. The Nakedness Of Noah 35
4. Jacob Wrestled With God 53
5. The Two Greatest Commandments 69
6. The Back Parts Of God 79
7. Moses Speaks Unadvisedly With His Lips 99
8. Blessings & Curses 107
9. Satan & The Anger Of The Lord 125
10. Jezebel Was Not A Whore 141
11. Death And Life 159
12. I Make Peace And Create Evil 175
13. No Weapon Formed Against Thee Shall Prosper 191
14. The Covenant With The Beasts, With The Fowls,
    And With The Creeping Things 211
Epilogue 229
About the Author 231

Preface

Receiving the Holy Ghost was the most amazing experience of my life. It was not amazing in a supernatural, out-of-body kind of way, but rather, amazing because I had been given a conscience that was not of this world: a conscience that would not allow me to be comforted by the unrestrained pursuit to fulfill my own selfish desire. With this newly formed conscience came another desire. A desire to understand who I had become and who I was supposed to be.

I was led to the Bible, and as I began to read, a feeling of joy came over me that I had never known before. But, soon thereafter, this feeling of joy was replaced with constant uncertainty. The Bible said a lot, but the Bible did not give my spirit that which I yearned for, so I continued to read, I continued to study, and I continued to pray. Finally, the Holy Ghost began to work his work: his strange work. The eyes of my understanding were opened, and I was introduced to a realm that I never imagined could exist. I thought I knew about God's word, but the Holy Ghost revealed to me how very little I knew about God's word in the way that I ought to know it. Although the Bible declares the will of God, it is the Spirit of God that teaches us the ways of the Father.

For many years I searched high and low for a guide to the truth. Even as a Christian, my thoughts were often plagued by the lack of understanding when it came to certain things that I read within the

Bible. I eventually learned that I did not even know how to read the Bible. As I attempted to climb out of darkness and into the religious world, I was introduced to a religious system that produced even more darkness, even more ideology, and even more self-righteousness; rarely did I find unfiltered truth. It was at this time in my life that I prayed to God and made a vow saying, "Lord, if you show me the truth of the scriptures, I promise you that I will declare the truth according to your desires and according to your wisdom."

So here we are. As a faithful servant of the Lord, I am proud to represent God's truth, God's whole truth, and nothing but God's truth. It is God's Spirit that allows the nature of Jesus Christ that dwells within our hearts to uncover the mysterious context of his word and reveal the heavenly dialect that escapes human comprehension. In PROVERBS 4:7, we were told by king Solomon, "Wisdom *is* the principal thing; *therefore*, get wisdom. And with all thy getting, get understanding." And thus, DIVINE CONTEXT (Vol. 1) is written for that sole purpose: understanding.

No matter how much we feel that we love God, we can never love our relationship with God unless we first learn to love the words that define the relationship that we share with God. We can never love the words that nourish our relationship with God unless we first understand those words. And we can never sincerely say that we love God's word until we sincerely understand God's word. Herein dwells the importance of Divine Context.

Introduction

Divine Context is the mysterious gates of heaven being unlocked so that the wisdom of God can enter our minds and settle our thoughts. Divine Context is the truth of what we think we know and the revelation of what we need to understand. DIVINE CONTEXT (Vol. 1) is a book of understanding that shines light on certain scriptures, particular events, and familiar situations that are within the Old Testament of the Bible. Although the substance of each scripture, event, and situation may have its origins within the Old Testament, the interpretations thereof are not entirely subjected to the Old Testament. In order to give precise detail to the revelation of each scripture, event, and situation, the entire Bible will be utilized for the purpose of revealing that the interpretations are of God and not of man.

The Old Testament is a shadow of the New, and the New Testament is the manifested glory that has always been hidden within the Old. Attempting to explain the Old Testament without the New Testament will only lead to uncertainty and debate. The Old Testament and the New Testament are the narrators of this book. Therefore, the interpretations thereof should not be accounted to man's wisdom, nor wisdom that is formulated to further one's own opinion. DIVINE CONTEXT (Vol. 1) is written to help settle our thoughts and reinforce our belief in God's word.

Each chapter of DIVINE CONTEXT (Vol. 1) will become a guiding light in the application of *context*. THE LIGHT THAT GOD CALLED **DAY** reveals how the sun was not the first light created by God. THE NAKEDNESS OF NOAH is a great example of how the scriptures can become a metaphorical maze that introduces an open door to the operation of interpretation that spans from one book to another. The universal authority of God is clearly recognized through SATAN AND THE ANGER OF THE LORD. JEZEBEL WAS NOT A WHORE will both surprise you and inform you at the same time. And NO WEAPON THAT IS FORMED AGAINST THEE SHALL PROSPER is a chapter that gives you a peek into the life story of the author himself.

A large portion of the Christian population assumes that the Holy Bible offers differing interpretations of the same scripture to multiple individuals. According to the Bible, this is not possible. For the possibility of truth to prevail, the *context* of the surrounding scriptures of a particular verse should become the foundation of what reveals the true meaning of that verse.

As we step into this journey of the spirit, we will be led by the Holy Ghost into a world where traditional religion cannot enter, where carnal wisdom cannot exist, and where the conversation of God opens itself up so that mankind can truly understand that God's ways are not our ways and that God's thoughts are not our thoughts. DIVINE CONTEXT (Vol. 1) is a book of understanding, a book of detailed direction, and a book that will help all maturing Christians grasp the depth of the word and the reality which reveals that the Old Testament is not a science fiction drama series that adds nothing to the New. Are you ready? If so, open your mind and your heart to receive the truth of the scripture and prepare your thoughts for the ride of Life. Amen!

Context #1 reveals that the first thing God created was his Word and how God separated the truth of his Word from all darkness.

GENESIS 1:1-5

1. IN the beginning God created the heaven and the earth.
2. And the earth was without form, and void; and darkness *was* upon the face of the deep. And the Spirit of God moved upon the face of the waters.
3. And God said, Let there be light: and there was light.
4. And God saw the light, that *it was* good: and God divided the light from the darkness.
5. And God called the light Day, and the darkness he called Night. And the evening and the morning were the first day.

The Light That God Called Day

Divine Context is understanding that the light that God divided from the darkness on the first day is not the radiance of the sun, the centerpiece of our solar system. On the contrary, the light that God called Day is the creation of God's word and the revelation that all things that exist are a product created by and under the authority of God's word.

* * *

When God said, "Let there be light . . . ," these four words had nothing to do with the shining of the sun on the earth or any other planet. The sun and the earth could have perhaps been created millions of years after this true light was established as the manufacturing element that will hold together and validate all that we see, understand, experience, and become.

The first light that was created on day one has nothing to do with the twenty-four-hour cycle that we call day, which represents one full rotation of the earth on its axis. According to Genesis 1:14-19, the sun, the moon, and the stars were all spoken into existence by God on day four of creation. The first thing that God created was the evidence and authority of his word. His word is separate from darkness, that is, separate from all that is not truth.

The first day of creation simply represents the first age of creation. The light of the first age is the creation of God's word and the establishment of the truth of God's word that is separate from all falsehood. The same word that God called Day is the same word that is separate from darkness. Regardless of the standard, the generation, or the era of time, the word of God will always represent light.

* * *

At the beginning of his ministry at the age of thirty, it is written that Jesus Christ spoke to the multitudes that were present, saying, "**Let your light so shine before men, that they may see your good works, and glorify your Father which is in heaven** [Mat. 5:16]." The only light that humans can allow to shine with purpose is the truth of God's word. The sun cannot produce nor inspire this light. God's light shines from within; God's light declares the bond of our unity with his divine plan. God's light is the example of our obedience to the truth of his word. No matter what generation or era, mankind's obedience to God's word has been an example of a shining light within our hearts and minds throughout all of history. Therefore, we should understand that the first light to shine on all things of creation is the word of God.

According to the first chapter in Genesis, God used his spoken word to create the sun, the moon, and the stars in age four of creation. With that being so, what else could this light be that was created in age one of creation other than God's word? The creating process and the creating authority of God's word are recognized throughout the first chapter of the book of Genesis. Genesis 1:3-31 show that God "said" a lot of things, and the expression of those sayings reveals to us that the light that God called Day is the tool that God used to bring all things of nature into existence.

* * *

It would be negligent to speak of the light that God called Day and not delve into the many fictional exploits that have been expressed concerning the origins and the existence of our Lord and Savior Jesus Christ, when it comes to the light that God called Day. Because of certain traditional religious doctrines, many Christians assume that it was Jesus Christ who created all the natural things of creation that we see and know. This assumption is based on New Testament scriptures such as 1 Corinthians 8:5-6, which speaks of all things being by Jesus Christ. When we use words or statements from any book or letter from the Bible, the central theme of the letter or book itself should be considered first and foremost. For example, Colossians 1:16-17 are words within a letter that the Apostle Paul wrote to the believers in Colosse, saying, **"For by him**(Jesus Christ) **were all things created, that are in heaven, and that are in earth, visible and invisible, whether *they be* thrones, or dominions, or principalities, or powers: all things were created by him, and for him: And he is before all things, and by him all things consist."**

If we attempt to interpret these words without first comprehending the central theme of Paul's letter to the Colossians, it would be easy for us to assume that it was Jesus Christ who created all things of nature and that Jesus Christ existed before anything was created. But the scripture of Colossians 1:16 does not say that Jesus Christ created all things of nature. The scripture says, "For by him were all things created, that are in heaven, and that are in earth. . . ." In order to understand the context of Colossians 1:16, we must not attempt to interpret the scripture based solely on identifying familiar words that are also documented in other parts of the Bible. The context of the surrounding scriptures of the letter of Colossians itself should be highly considered when interpreting Colossians 1:16-17.

By explaining the creating powers of Jesus Christ using Paul's letter to the Colossians, let us first identify the subject matter of the letter of Colossians. The letter of Colossians was written to Christian disciples many years after Christ's ministry, Christ's death on the cross, and Christ's resurrection from the dead. The disciples of Jesus Christ had become slack in their efforts to obey God's will according to the example of Jesus Christ that reflects God's righteousness. The righteous example of Jesus Christ is the life that Jesus Christ lived before God according to the gospel of Matthew, Mark, Luke, and John. Only one question appears in the letter of Colossians. In Colossians 2:20-22 the Apostle Paul asked this question, "**Wherefore if ye**(your sinful nature) **be dead with Christ from the rudiments of the world, why, as though living in the world, are ye**(your renewed nature) **subject to ordinances**(rules)**, (Touch not; taste not; handle not; Which all are to perish with the using;) after the commandments and doctrines of men?**" Based on Colossians 2:20-22, although the disciples of Christ believed in Jesus, some of them were beginning to follow the gospel of Jesus Christ based on manmade teachings that were being created by corrupt individuals who were claiming to belong to the Christian faith.

When the scriptures of Colossians 1:16-17 speaks of all the thrones, all the dominions, all the principalities, and all the powers in heaven and in earth being created by Jesus Christ, and Jesus being before all things, these words are only a continuing statement from what Paul wrote earlier in chapter one of Colossians. Within the scripture of Colossians 1:8, Paul spoke of the love that the Colossians held in their hearts towards Jesus Christ. But despite their faith in Jesus Christ, some of them were following manmade doctrines and falling short of the example of Jesus Christ. Their efforts in the gospel were not reflecting the obedient example of the testimony that Christ created to be placed within their hearts. At the beginning of his letter, Colossians 1:9-12 shows that Paul spoke of his prayers and his desires for the Colossians, saying, "**For this cause we**(Paul and his Christian companions) **also, since the day we heard** *it*(*your love*)**, do not cease to pray for you, and to desire that ye might be filled with the knowledge**(acknowledgement) **of his**(Christ's) **will in all wisdom and spiritual understanding; That ye might walk worthy of the Lord unto all pleasing, being fruitful in every good work, and increasing in the knowledge**(acknowledgement) **of God**(God's will)**; Strengthened with all might, according to his**(Christ's) **glorious power, unto all patience and longsuffering with joyfulness; Giving thanks unto the Father, which hath made us meet**(qualified) **to be partakers of the**

inheritance of the saints in light. . . ." As born-again Christians, God has allowed us to inherit a portion of Christ's character, which gives us our callings; that is, our thrones, dominion, principalities, and powers within the body of Christ according to Ephesians 4:4-16 also.

The reason the Colossians could now gain the ability to acknowledge Christ's will in all wisdom and in all spiritual understanding is because of the testimony that Jesus Christ fulfilled. The spiritual callings that are distributed among the believers were not created because of the life that Jesus lived as a carpenter up until the age of thirty. It was the three-year ministry in which Jesus manifested as the anointed one that enabled the callings of the body of Christ to be created and distributed among his believers. Hebrews 8:8-11 teaches us that it is because of the ministry of Jesus Christ that the disciples of Christ now have the inheritance of Christ's righteousness placed within our hearts and minds. For this reason, in the first chapter of Colossians, Paul continued to speak of the power of God and the effects of the righteousness of Christ by saying, "**Who**(God) **hath delivered us from the power of darkness, and hath translated**(transformed) ***us* into the kingdom**(body) **of his dear Son: In whom**(Christ) **we have redemption through his**(Christ's) **blood**(righteousness)**, *even* the forgiveness of sins: . . .** [Col. 1:13-14]." The power of the Holy Ghost not only delivers us from darkness, which is falsehood and ignorance, but the Holy Ghost also transforms our hearts so that we can begin to manifest the characteristics of the Son of God. It is the characteristics of the Son of God that is placed within our hearts and gives us the ability to manifest our spiritual gifts and our spiritual callings. All the callings of the New Testament era were created by the testimony of Jesus Christ and for the testimony of Jesus Christ.

* * *

Once we grasp that the context of Colossians 1:16-17 is speaking in terms of all things of the New Testament era being created by the ministry of Jesus, we can begin to identify the precise creating powers of Jesus Christ. Nevertheless, one could then question the divinity of

Jesus Christ. Is Jesus Christ God himself in the flesh? To disobey Jesus Christ would be the same as disobeying God. In the twelfth chapter of the gospel, according to Saint John, Jesus told the Jews that the same word that he spoke to them would be the word that would judge them in the end (John 12:48). And then Jesus said, "**For I have not spoken of myself; but the Father which sent me, he gave me a commandment, what I should say, and what I should speak. And I know that his commandment is life everlasting: whatsoever I speak therefore, even as the Father said unto me, so I speak** [John 12:49-50]." The revelation that Jesus was subject to God does not take away from Christ's divinity. The divinity of Jesus Christ was confirmed through his obedience to God. Therefore, Paul wrote to the Colossians about how Christ's disciples could obtain redemption from sin through Christ's blood, which blood represents righteousness.

In Colossians 1:15-17 Paul continued to build on the righteous character of Jesus Christ, saying, "**Who**(Christ's righteousness) **is the image**(representation) **of the invisible God, the firstborn**(first to be born again by receiving the Holy Ghost) **of every creature**(New Testament disciple)**: For by him**(Christ's righteousness) **were all things created, that are in heaven**(God's will according to the New Testament)**, and that are in earth**(the hearts and minds of the New Testament disciples)**, visible**(that which can be comprehended) **and invisible**(that which had not been comprehended as of yet)**, whether** *they be* **thrones**(positions within the body of Christ)**, or dominions**(callings that require some to have authority over others)**, or principalities**(religious leaders)**, or powers**(spiritual gifts)**: all things were created by him**(Christ's righteousness)**, and for him**(Christ's righteousness)**: And he**(Christ's righteousness) **is before**(above) **all things, and by him**(Christ's righteousness) **all things consist.** Was the physical body of Jesus the image of the invisible God? Ask yourself that question.

God is Spirit. When the scripture speaks of Jesus being in the image of the invisible God, the word invisible represents mankind's inability to comprehend God's eternal will. Without the Holy Ghost, the righteousness of God that is revealed through the testimony of Jesus

Christ cannot be comprehended, thus making it invisible to the carnal mind. Therefore, the only image that Jesus Christ could bear concerning the invisible God is the representation of God's righteous will that was being expressed through Christ's obedience (Heb. 5:8-9). Christ's obedience is the same image of obedience that the New Testament disciples are expected to strive for among one another.

All things were indeed created by Jesus Christ and for Jesus Christ. But the things that have been created by Christ and for Christ are not the natural hosts of heaven and earth, such as the planets that fill the universe, the sun, the moon, the stars, the grass, the trees, the birds, the fish, and the wild animals of the fields. The creating powers of Jesus Christ were given to him when he was first baptized by John the Baptist and received the gift of the Holy Ghost from God at about the age of thirty (Luke 3:21-23). The baptism of Jesus Christ signified the beginning of Christ's three-year ministry (John 2:11) and the beginning of a new generation of believers that would become God's new and improved holy nation (Mat. 9:14-17).

The letter of Colossians is written to give us an example of how it is the righteousness of Christ within our hearts that transforms us from sinful creatures into obedient servants of God. Within the third chapter of Colossians, Paul speaks of how before the disciples of Christ inherit Christ's righteousness, we all walk in disobedience (Col. 3:5-7). Then Paul says, "**But now ye also put off all these; anger, wrath, malice, blasphemy, filthy**(shameful) **communication out of your mouth** [Col. 3:8]." Paul goes on to say, "**Lie not one to another, seeing that ye have put off the old**(sinful) **man**(nature) **with his deeds; And have put on the new**(obedient) ***man(nature)*, which is renewed in knowledge after the image**(representation) **of him**(Christ's righteousness) **that created him: Where there is neither Greek**(Gentile) **nor Jew, circumcision**(Jew) **nor uncircumcision**(Gentile)**, Barbarian**(foreigner)**, Scythian**(savage)**, bond *nor* free: but Christ**(Christ's righteousness) ***is*** **all, and in all** [Col. 3:9-11]." The new spiritual character that all born-again Christians inherit is the creation of the righteousness of Jesus Christ: the righteousness that Jesus Christ represented during his three-year ministry here on earth.

Paul desired the Colossians to recognize that within the New Testament era, the thrones (positions within the body of Christ), the dominions (callings that required having authority over others), the principalities (religious leaders), and the powers (spiritual gifts) were all created by the testimony of Jesus Christ. Each of these elements within the body of Christ eventually becomes apparent to us once we receive the gift of the Holy Ghost. These are the things that were created by Jesus and represent the characteristics and righteousness of Jesus Christ.

The righteousness of Jesus was fulfilled through the manifestation of Christ's three-year ministry, but the creation of the three-year ministry of Jesus Christ was declared by God long before Jesus was conceived in the womb of Mary, long before Jesus was born in the manger, long before Jesus became a carpenter, and long before Jesus received the Holy Ghost. The testimony of Jesus, the anointed one, became a creation of God immediately after the fall of Adam (Gen. 3:12-15). After Adam and Eve's disobedience, then the prophecies of Jesus Christ were declared by most of the Old Testament prophets. Christian wisdom, Christian knowledge, Christian faith, Christian belief, Christian understanding, Christian endurance, Christian temperance, Christian gifts of healing, Christian gifts of preaching, Christian gifts of teaching, and Christian gifts of prophesying are all elements within the Christian experience that were created when Jesus fulfilled his ministry as Jesus the anointed one.

All these spiritual attributes were displayed and established by Jesus Christ from the very beginning of his ministry. Jesus Christ created a new way of life according to a new standard that was put in place by God. All the things that pertain to the life and spiritual gifts that are created by the righteousness of Jesus Christ are judged according to Christ's standard of righteousness within the New Testament. Through the baptism of the Holy Ghost, Jesus Christ was given the ability to create gifts that gave his disciples their position and their purpose within the body of Christ.

Moreover, the gifts and the callings that men and women receive as Christians were created through the example of Jesus Christ. Those gifts and those callings were also created to be a witness for Christ's testimony. All the spiritual ability and all the spiritual authority that we receive as

Christians through our callings are a direct result of the testimony that Jesus Christ achieved as the Messiah of the New Covenant.

The mystery of how the disciples of Jesus Christ received their callings was a hidden truth for many years. Therefore, when the creating influences of Jesus Christ began to manifest itself within the hearts of the New Testament disciples, Paul revealed the mystery of how these abilities would come about. By referring to his very own ministry, Paul concluded the first chapter of Colossians by stating that his calling as a minister of Christ was to make known to the Gentiles the mystery that had been hidden from other generations (Col. 1:25-29). And what is that mystery? In the words of the Apostle Paul, the mystery "**. . . is Christ in you, the hope of glory . . .** [Col. 1:27]."

Because of the commandments and doctrines of certain men who were perverting the gospel of Christ, the first-century disciples of the New Testament were failing to manifest God's righteousness according to the characteristics of Jesus Christ. This is the reason why the central theme of the letter of Colossians is focused on Christ's righteousness. It is Christ's righteousness that created our callings and our positions in the church. Christ's righteousness comes before our callings, and it is because of Christ's righteousness that our callings exist.

* * *

It was Jesus Christ who proclaimed that he was the light of life (John 8:12). Therefore, I once believed that Jesus Christ was the light that was in the beginning with God because John begins his gospel by saying, "**IN the beginning was the Word, and the Word was with God, and the Word was God** [John 1:1]." It was easy for my carnal mind to assume that the light in Genesis 1:3-4 was referring to Jesus because he said that he is the light. In the first verse of the gospel, according to Saint John, it is evident that the word "beginning" refers to the beginning of creation. There are times, however, when the word "beginning" is mentioned in the New Testament that we must understand its context as pertaining to the beginning of Christ's three-year ministry, as opposed to the beginning of creation referred to in the Old Testament book of

Genesis. This is not always the case, but there are a few examples of the word "beginning" referring to the beginning of Christ ministry (Mark 1:1 / John 2:11/15:27 / 1 John 1:1-3).

When we come across the word "beginning" in the New Testament, we rarely think of the beginning of Christ's three-year ministry. We often allow our minds to think back to the book of Genesis without considering the overall context of the letter which we are reading at that very moment. For example, when we read the scriptures of Colossians that say all things were created by Jesus Christ and that Jesus Christ is before all things (Col. 1:16-17), we must also consider that the subject matter of the letter to the Colossians focuses on the authority that the righteousness of Jesus Christ has over all the things that belong to Christianity. As the New Testament principles and gifts were created by the righteous example of Jesus Christ, even so, is the manifestation of Christ's righteousness the standard that we should strive for in the New Testament. Through our collective manifestation of Christ's righteousness, all that pertains to the New Testament will come together perfectly. Christ's righteousness should be the beginning of all that we become. Christ's righteousness should be the first principle in all that we seek to achieve. It is because of Christ's righteousness that we belong to the family of the New Testament.

The righteousness of Christ is the true light for all to follow as the example of what God desires of us according to the New Testament. Nevertheless, Jesus Christ himself had nothing to do with creating the light that God called Day at the beginning of creation. Our Lord does bear the image of light, which is to say that Jesus Christ bears the image of God's righteousness through his testimony. In all honesty, the image of the righteousness of Jesus Christ was subsequently formed by the light(word) that God called Day.

When the religious elite brought to Jesus a woman who had been caught in the act of adultery, they attempted to find fault in Jesus by trying to see if he would say things contrary to the Old Testament law. Jesus did not condemn the woman, nor did Jesus allow the men that brought her before him to do so either. Through his words, Jesus persuaded the men who brought the woman before him to look at themselves and recognize that, just like the woman, they also were sinners. Rising above the traditional standard of the Old Testament law, Jesus Christ then goes on to say to them all, "**I am the light**(example) **of the world: he that followeth me shall not walk in darkness**(ignorance)**, but shall have the light**(example) **of life** [John 8:12]." Although Jesus, at that moment, confessed that he was now the light of life, his light was not the example that God commanded the Jews in the Old Testament to live by.

Within the Old and the New Testament, there are four stages of light that are revealed through the testimonies of certain individuals who were called by God in order to restore the righteousness that Adam failed to maintain. After the fall of Adam, the light of sacrifice was established by Moses (Lev. 9); then, the prophets of the Old Testament up until John the Baptist established the light of repentance (Mat. 11:13). After John the Baptist, Jesus from the age of thirty to thirty-three established the light of righteousness (Rom. 3:21-26). Finally, the apostles of Jesus Christ, including the Apostle Paul, established the light of order through their testimonies (1 Cor. 11:34/14:40).

In the beginning of man's existence, Adam, the first human being, manifested the light of eternal righteousness by obeying the will of God and not eating of the tree of the knowledge of good and evil. Before Adam disobeyed God's word, his example of obedience was the righteous example of God's will. God's words represent God's will, and God's will represents God.

In his attempt to explain the far-reaching authority of God's word, the Apostle John began his gospel by saying, "**IN the beginning was the Word**(will of God)**, and the Word**(will of God) **was with God, and the Word**(will of God) **was**(represented) **God. The same was in the beginning with God. All things were made by him**(the will of God)**; and without him**(the will of God) **was not anything made that was made** [John 1:1-3]." Regardless of the human era in which it exists and regardless of the standard that is established thereby, the same word that represents God's will is the same word that God used to speak all things of nature into existence. This is the same word that would keep Adam mindful of God's spoken will.

Is it correct to say that Jesus Christ was in the beginning with God and that Jesus Christ was the light that God called Day? If so, think of this. The righteous example of Jesus Christ did not exist for Adam to accept and follow. Nevertheless, Adam did follow the presence of God's spoken word, which reminded Adam not to eat of the tree of the knowledge of good and evil (Gen. 2:16-17).

To assume that Jesus Christ existed before the New Testament in any form other than a proposed prophesy would be to falsify the birth of Jesus in the manger and suggest that the thirty-three-years of Jesus' life was a display of deception. And to believe that God allowed the physical manifestation of Jesus Christ to appear before his testimony within the New Testament would also be to falsify the birth of Jesus in the manger and suggest that the thirty-three-years of Jesus' life was a display of deception. No matter how we may consider certain situations within the Old Testament to justify that the life of Jesus Christ existed before the New Testament, we must acknowledge that the physical existence of Jesus and the ministry of Jesus Christ is the reality of the documented life of Jesus Christ: the gospels of Matthew, Mark, Luke, and John.

Although the impending life of Jesus Christ was spoken of many times beforehand by the Old Testament prophets, the physical existence of Jesus and the expressed life of Jesus as the anointed one was not the standard that the Old Testament generations were justified by. They were justified by the law of Moses. Even Jesus Christ himself understood that his followers could not be justified in the New Covenant until his testimony was complete. Therefore, as he taught his disciples about the new covenant, he also said to them, "**Think not that I am come to destroy the law, or the prophets: I am not come to destroy, but to fulfil. For verily I say unto you, Till heaven**(the law of Moses) **and earth**(natural birthright) **pass**(be excluded)**, one jot or one tittle shall in no wise pass**(be excluded) **from the law, till all be fulfille**d [Mat. 5:17-18]." All the prophecies concerning the life of Jesus were fulfilled when he died on the cross, and God raised him from the dead.

When Jesus died and rose, it was at this point that the law of Moses and the birthright of an Israelite became excluded as the standard to be God's chosen people. Now that title would belong to all those who believe in Jesus regardless of what race they were born into (John 1:11-13). This is what the prophet Isaiah meant when he wrote, "**For behold, I**(God) **create new heavens and a new earth: that the former**(law of Moses & the ministry of the prophets) **shall not be remembered, nor come into mind** [Isa. 65:17]." The word "heavens" in Isaiah 65:17 represent the two distinctive foundations that solidify the New Testament: the righteousness of Jesus Christ and the order of the Apostle's ministry. The "former" would be the old heavens, which represent Moses (the law of sacrifice) and the Prophets (the ministry of Repentance).

The word of God that was birthed into existence long before the testimony of Jesus Christ was the same light that Adam used to comprehend the path that God desired for him. Once Adam behaved in a manner that was contrary to God's word and chose to eat of the tree of the knowledge of good and evil, Adam's soul entered darkness because of his disobedience. On the path to restoring the former example of Adam's manifestation of righteousness, God first implemented the law of Moses and the testimony of the prophets who followed Moses as his perfect will for the Old Testament era (Rom. 5:12-14). The law of Moses and the testimony of the prophets introduced the light of sacrifice and the light of repentance. Anyone choosing to obey the law of Moses would be considered righteous in the sight of God according to the law of sacrifice (Luke 1:5-6).

All the Old Testament prophets begged the children of Israel to return their hearts to God and obey the law that was given to Moses (Jer. 25:1-7). When Jesus Christ spoke to his disciples about John the Baptist, he referred to John the Baptist as a bright and shining light that the Jews were willing to rejoice in for a season (John 5:32-35). But John the Baptist acknowledged that his light had to decrease so that the light of Jesus Christ could increase (John 3:28-31). John the Baptist was the last Old Testament prophet (Mat. 11:12-13). And in the tradition of every Old Testament prophet, Luke 3:3 says, "**And he**(John the Baptist) **came into all the country about Jordan**(the Jordan River), **preaching the baptism of repentance for the remission of sins. . . .**"

After the light of repentance, God used Jesus to establish the light of righteousness, which would be the true reformation of the righteousness that Adam forsook. The words, the works, and the suffering of Jesus Christ are the new example of light that restored eternal life. The righteousness of Jesus Christ is the light that John the Baptist said was coming after repentance but is preferred before repentance (John 1:29-31). This is to say that the word of eternal righteousness that was once declared to Adam came before the word of sacrifice and repentance that was declared by Moses and the Old Testament prophets; although in Jesus Christ, the process to restore the light of eternal righteousness comes after the lights of sacrifice and repentance.

In the case of Jesus Christ, the word of God was made flesh in the glory "as of" the only begotten Son of God (John 1:14). The word was not made flesh in the glory "as of" a servant of God. The word that was in the beginning with God, which word God gave to Adam, is the same word that Jesus Christ was created to restore. Therefore, it is said that ". . . **the Word**(will of God) **was made flesh**(the testimony of Jesus Christ)**, and dwelt among us**(the apostles) . . . [John 1:14]**."** The word was made flesh indeed, but not in the manner that our carnal minds consider.

The word of God being made flesh is spoken of in the context of Jesus Christ manifesting the documented prophecies of his ministry that were written beforehand in the Old Testament. John 1:14 is not referring to Jesus' conception in the womb of Mary or the birth of Jesus in the manger. The first chapter of the gospel of John has nothing to do with the birth of Jesus. The context of the first chapter of John's gospel was written in the past tense, focusing on the Messiah's introduction to the Jews through Christ's ministry. The first chapter in the gospel according to John, is the example of Jesus being baptized with the Holy Ghost and becoming one with the prophecies concerning himself (Luke 24:44-45).

It was the former prophecies that could now be made flesh through the life of Jesus once he began to establish himself as the anointed one. There is no portion of John's gospel that speaks of the introduction of Jesus' fleshly body into the world through birth. In the fourteenth verse of the first chapter of John's gospel, John says, "**And the Word**(Old Testament prophecies) **was made flesh**(the testimony of Jesus Christ)**, and dwelt among us**(the apostles)**, (and we**(the apostles) **beheld** his(Christ's) **glory, the glory as of the only begotten of the Father,) full of grace and truth** [John 1:14]." Neither the Apostle John nor any of the other apostles, nor any of the other disciples, were present with Joseph and Mary in the manger when Jesus was born (Luke 2:7-20). Therefore, the only glory that they could have beheld of Jesus Christ was the carpenter manifesting his transformation into the Messiah at the age of thirty. Jesus Christ was no more the quiet carpenter after he was baptized by John the Baptist and received the Holy Ghost. Jesus began to proclaim the gospel of the New Testament by teaching in many of the local synagogues (Luke 4:14-15). This is what Christ's disciples beheld. John and the other apostles were there in the presence of Jesus Christ and beheld Christ's transformation at the beginning of his ministry as the Holy Ghost manifested the change that had come alive within him.

The ministry of Jesus Christ reveals the difference between the light of righteousness and the light of sacrifice and repentance. Jesus did not begin his ministry as a servant, ignorant of all that he would go through. After receiving the Holy Ghost, Jesus stepped forward as the Messiah, wise and mindful of who he was and aware of the change that had taken place within him (John 4:25-26). Jesus Christ understood the course of events that he would face during the next three years of his life. This revelation was not fully brought alive within Jesus until after he was baptized in the Jordan River by John the Baptist and received the Holy Spirit (Acts 10:36-38). Therefore, it is important to understand that "the Word" being made flesh was spoken of in the perfect context of the ministry of Jesus Christ, as opposed to the context of Jesus' physical birth by the virgin Mary. The light of the law of sacrifice was given to Moses between the ages of eighty and one hundred and twenty (Exo. 7:7 / Deu. 34:7). The manifestation of the light of eternal righteousness revealed itself once again in Jesus Christ between the ages of thirty and thirty-three.

The light of righteousness came from Jesus Christ for the example of a new way of life for all that would believe in Christ's light. Christ's example is the brightest light of all that came before him, or that would come after him. As says the scripture, "**Thou**(Christ) **lovest**(loves) **righteousness, and hatest**(hates) **wickedness: therefore God, thy**

God, hath(has) **anointed thee with the oil of gladness above thy fellows**(associates) [Psa. 45:7]." Christ's testimony is above sacrifice and repentance.

Now, if we choose to accept the example(light) of Jesus Christ according to our own self-righteousness, the light that is within us remains darkened. Our darkness then becomes a light unto ourselves, and unfortunately, our self-righteousness is the one light that is separated from the eternal will of God. During his sermon on the mountain, Jesus spoke to the multitudes about the treasures of the heart, saying, "**The light of the body is the eye**(vision)**: if therefore thine eye**(vision) **be single**(clear)**, thy whole body shall be full of light. But if thine eye**(vision) **be evil, thy whole body shall be full of darkness**(falsehood)**. If therefore the light that** *is* **in thee be darkness**(false)**, how great** *is* **that darkness**(falsehood) [Mat. 6:22-23]!"

* * *

In the beginning of creation, God's word is called light. God's word all alone is the light that God called Day. The testimony of Jesus Christ was not present with God in the beginning of creation. Nevertheless, the Bible reveals that within God's light, we have multiple degrees of brightness based on the different generations in which God's word has been received and obeyed by mankind. The testimony of Jesus Christ is the brightest of all lights. The light of Christ is the example of Adam, without the transgression (Rom. 5:12-19). According to the standard of the New Testament, everything that is sincere, pure, honest, lovely, enduring, and of a good report was created by the testimony of Jesus Christ. Although Christ's testimony was not the light of the first day, over a period of thousands of years, Christ's long-awaited testimony was created by the light of the first day. Once the testimony of Christ became reality, then it was through his obedience to God's word that his testimony created all that we can become as the disciples of the new covenant.

The most effective instrument that our God uses to communicate with mankind is his very first creation; his word. The word of God possesses the ability to enlighten our minds and hearts on a level that the sunlight can never reach. This is the same word that God used to create heaven, earth, the sun, the moon, the stars, the trees, the vegetation of the ground, the animals of the fields, and mankind. Before the word of God could accomplish all these amazing things, God had to first create and establish his word. The word(light) that God called Day is the same word that God separated from darkness (Gen. 1:4-5). It is the same word that gives us truth(light): the same word that separates us from falsehood(darkness). Aside from every other earthly element, every other heavenly host, and every other living being, the light that God called Day in the first era of creation is most definitely the power and authority of God's word. The light that God called Day has just been revealed in Divine Context.

Context #2 reveals how God created all things of nature in six consecutive eras, as opposed to God creating all things of nature in six consecutive twenty-four-hour cycles.

GENESIS 1:31-2:1-3

31. And God saw every thing that he had made, and, behold, *it was* very good. And the evening and the morning were the sixth day.
1. THUS the heavens and the earth were finished, and all the host of them.
2. And on the seventh day God ended his work which he had made; and he rested on the seventh day from all his work which he had made.
3. And God blessed the seventh day, and sanctified it: because that in it he had rested from all his work which God created and made.

The Six Days Of Creation

*   *   *

Divine Context is understanding that when God declared to the people of Israel that he created all that we see and experience of nature in six days, God was not literally speaking of six consecutive twenty-four cycles.

*   *   *

Within the first day of creation, God established his word as the creating instrument that would give life and purpose to all that we see and experience of nature (Gen. 1:2-5 / John 1:1-3). Then the scripture says, "**And the evening and the morning were the first day** [Gen. 1:5]."

Within the second day of creation, God used his word to create the Heavenly expanse (Gen. 1:6-8). And then the scripture says, "**And the evening and the morning were the second day** [Gen. 1:8]."

Within the third day of creation, God used his word to create Earth (Gen. 1:9-10) and all the plant life which decorates the earth's surface, saying, "**Let the earth bring forth grass, the herb yielding seed, *and* the fruit tree yielding fruit after his kind, whose seed *is* in itself, upon the earth: and it was so** [Gen. 1:11]." And then the scripture says, "**And the evening and the morning were the third day** [Gen. 1:13]."

Within the fourth day of creation, God used his word to create the sun, the moon, and the stars (Gen. 1:14-18). And then the scripture says, "**And the evening and the morning were the fourth day** [Gen. 1:19]."

Within the fifth day of creation, God used his word to create the birds that fly through the skies above earth, and the living marine life that dwells within the oceans, the seas, and the lakes of earth (Gen. 1:20-22). And then the scripture says, "**And the evening and the morning were the fifth day** [Gen. 1:23]."

Within the sixth day of creation, God used his word to create a human being and called his name Adam. Also, within this sixth day of creation, God used his word to create the cattle of the field and all the animals that creep on the ground in an attempt to find a companion that would be compatible with the man that he had created (Gen. 1:24-25 / 2:7-20). God finally used man's own body to create a woman (Gen. 2:20-23). And then the scripture says, "**And the evening and the morning were the sixth day** [Gen. 1:31]."

In six consecutive days, God created the authority of his word, the heavenly expanse, the earthly boundaries, the sun, the moon, the stars, the fowls of the air, the marine life that inhabits the waters of earth, a man, the animals of the field, and a woman. Then the scripture says, "**THUS the heavens and the earth were finished, and all the host**(resources) **of them. And on the seventh day God ended his work which he had made; and he rested on the seventh day from all his work which he had made. And God blessed the seventh day, and sanctified it: because that in it he had rested from all his work which God created and made** [Gen. 2:1-3]."

* * *

The events that take place on the fourth day of creation will help us to understand that God created all things of nature in six consecutive eras, as opposed to God creating all things of nature in six consecutive twenty-four-hour cycles. In the fourth era of creation, God used his word to create the sun, the moon, and the stars. God then said that the sun, the moon, and the stars would "**. . . be for signs, and for seasons,**

and for days, and years . . . [Gen. 1:14]." God called the sun the greater light, and he called the moon the lesser light. These are the lights that instituted the twenty-four-hour cycle that mankind acknowledges as night and day. Before the fourth era of creation, one full rotation of the earth on its axis was not considered a period of twenty-four hours because of the absence of the sun, the moon, and the stars. Before the sun, the moon, and the stars were created by God, the earth itself did not experience seasons, days, or years. The fourth day(era of creation) is what constitutes the twenty-four-hour cycle.

Moreover, even without the presence of the sun, the moon, and the stars, Moses still referred to the creation of God's word as ". . . the first day," the creation of the heavenly void as ". . . the second day," and the creation of earth's solid foundation as ". . . the third day." Each day represents an era in which God created something of nature, established something of nature, and completed the functioning of something of nature.

The words "evening" and "morning," which appear within the first chapter of Genesis, are the keys to understanding that there was a process of completion at the end of each era. Evening comes before morning at the completion of each separate creation. The word "evening" is directed towards the ending of an era that God has completed. The word "morning" is directed towards another era that is now in the process of its beginning. There could not have been a second era of creation until the first era of creation had been completed. Similarly, there could not have been a third era of creation until the second era of creation had been completed, and so on unto the sixth era of creation.

We are now in the seventh era. We cannot call this era an era of creation. We can only call this era an era of complete existence. In this seventh era, all that has been spoken into existence from era one through era six come together as a carefully crafted mystery, with a variety of elements that are impossible for mankind to stop or hinder. Before the creation of mankind, the five previous eras of nature had already taken their course for the purpose of sustaining human and animal life forms. Once God created the human life form and the animals of the field, God then ended his external work of creating. Mankind and the animal kingdom were the final pieces to the puzzle that gave divine purpose to the universe, which was already set in motion. The seventh era has been proceeding forward as we know it ever since, for at the end of the sixth day(era), it is said, "**THUS the heavens and the earth were finished, and all the host**(resources) **of them. And on the seventh day God ended his work which he had made; and he rested on the seventh day from all his work which he had made. And God blessed the seventh day**(era of existence)**, and sanctified it: because that in it he had rested from all his work which God created and made** [Gen. 2:1-3]."

In this seventh era of existence, the discoveries that have come about through the power of God have been assisted by the knowledge and wisdom that God has given to mankind. Mankind does not have the ability to create something new except through the discoveries of the things that have already been created by God (Ecc. 1:3-9). Unfortunately, within this seventh era, all the rebellion, all the evil, all the murder, all the covetousness, all the wickedness, all the pride, all the deceitfulness, all the envy, and all the falsehood have been discovered through the assistance of man's imagination (Rom. 1:28-31 / Gal. 5:19-21). Fortunately, mankind has also been given the chance to discover love, joy, peace, patience, tolerance, charity, gentleness, goodness, meekness, and faith through the assistance of man's imagination in this seventh era of existence (Gal. 5:22-23). It is not written within the Bible that this seventh era has an evening; therefore, we would assume, unless otherwise proven false, that the evening of the seventh era on earth for each human being will come to pass when we die.

The fall of Adam and Eve and the rise of Jesus Christ have all taken place within this seventh era of existence. Nothing new has been created outside of the capabilities of the human body and mind. God finished his work of creating new external things of nature at the end of the sixth era of creation. But after the transgression of Adam, within this seventh era of existence, God began his internal work of restoring the righteousness of mankind with this first prophecy concerning judgment towards Satan, saying, "**Because thou**(the serpent) **hast done this** (deceived Eve)**, thou *art* cursed above all cattle, and above every beast of the** field; upon thy belly shalt thou go, and dust shalt thou eat all the days of thy life: And I will put enmity(hatred) **between thee and the woman, and between thy seed and her seed; it shall bruise thy head, and thou shalt bruise his heel** [Gen. 3:14-15]."

In this seventh era of existence, God rested from all his solitary works, and then after the fall of Adam, God began the work of assisting mankind by using mankind to recover the righteousness that was lost through the transgression of Adam. In the same manner, because the restoration of eternal righteousness has now been fulfilled through our Lord Jesus Christ, God is asking Christ's disciples to rest from their own works in this seventh era and assist him in the conformation of the eternal righteousness that has now been revived and restored.

Within the letter to the Hebrews, the author wrote of the children of Israel's failure to believe in God and forsake their own ways when they were delivered out of the land of Egypt. Their failure resulted in a whole generation having to wander in the wilderness for forty years. The children of Israel's example of unbelief is a direct warning to Christ's disciples who fail to forsake their own self-righteousness. Paul says, "**For he that is entered into his**(God's) **rest**(abode)**, he also hath ceased from his own works, as God** *did* **from his. Let us labour therefore to enter into that**(God's) **rest, lest any man fall after the same**(children of Israel's) **example of unbelief** [Heb. 4:10-11]."

* * *

Genesis 1:1 says, "**IN the beginning God created the heaven and the earth.**" The first verse of the book of Genesis represents the six collective eras of creation. When we read the book of Exodus, where God gives the children of Israel the Ten Commandments, the fourth commandment says, "**Remember the sabbath day, to keep it holy. Six days shalt thou labour, and do all thy work: But the seventh day** *is* **the sabbath of the LORD thy God:** *in it* **thou shalt not do any work, thou, nor thy son, nor thy daughter, thy manservant, nor thy maidservant, nor thy cattle, nor thy stranger that** *is* **within thy gates: For** *in* **six days the LORD made heaven and earth, the sea, and all that in them** *is,*

and rested the seventh day: wherefore the LORD blessed the sabbath day, and hallowed it [Exo. 20:8-11]."

The scriptures of Exodus 20:8-11 are the words that many use to affirm that God created all things within six days. The twenty-four-hour cycle that mankind experiences was created in the fourth era of creation when God created the sun, the moon, and the stars. Then God said concerning the sun, the moon, and the stars, "**. . . let them be for signs, and for seasons, and for days, and years . . .** [Gen. 1:14]." Mankind refers to the twenty-four-hour cycle that God created in the fourth era of creation as a day. But for God, the twenty-four-hour cycle that mankind experiences are a microsecond within his day. It could have taken millions, maybe even billions of man-years, to shape the universe in a manner that the earth could remain capable of sustaining human life as we experience it today.

The Apostle Peter was no stranger to this revelation. In his second letter to Christians, Peter spoke of the day of the Lord that was to come. Peter said that there would be those who would begin to question the Lord's coming because of all the years that have come and gone after Christ's resurrection (2 Pet. 3:1-4). For this reason, Peter then says to Christ's disciples, "**But, beloved, be not ignorant of this one thing, that one day *is* with the Lord as a thousand years, and a thousand years as one day** [2 Pet. 3:8]." The six days of creation spoken of in the book of Genesis are six consecutive eras that God used to create and bring into being all that exists.

The six days(eras) of creation are all unique and distinctive in how God expressed the authority of his word and his creative imagination. The planet earth that we live on, and the universe that we inhabit, are living organisms of nature itself. They speak to us in many beautiful and destructive ways. We all know that with God anything is possible, but we must understand that God's creation of nature did not come about in the period of one hundred and forty-four hours. The six days of creation have just been revealed in Divine Context.

Context #3 reveals how Noah was misled by following the people and how his two sons Shem and Japheth helped Noah to recognize his error.

GENESIS 9:18-27

18. And the sons of Noah, that went forth of the ark, were Shem, and Ham, and Japheth: and Ham *is* the Father of Canaan.
19. These *are* the three sons of Noah: and of them was the whole earth overspread.
20. And Noah began *to be* an husbandman, and he planted a vineyard:
21. And he drank of the wine, and was drunken; and he was uncovered within his tent.
22. And Ham, the father of Canaan, saw the nakedness of his father, and told his two brethren without.
23. And Shem and Japheth took a garment, and laid *it* upon both their shoulders, and went backward, and covered the nakedness of their father; and their faces *were* backward, and they saw not their father's nakedness.
24. And Noah awoke from his wine, and knew what his younger son (Ham) had done unto him.
25. And he said, Cursed *be* Canaan; a servant of servants shall he be unto his brethren.
26. And he(Noah) said, Blessed *be* the LORD God of Shem; and Canaan shall be his servant.
27. God shall enlarge Japheth, and he shall dwell in the tents of Shem; and Canaan shall be his servant.

The Nakedness Of Noah

Divine Context is understanding that Noah's nakedness should not be interpreted literally as nudity in the sense that Noah's penis and his buttocks had been exposed during the encounter with his son Ham.

* * *

The nakedness of Noah has been spoken of in a variety of ways among believers, young and old. The first time that I read these few verses of the Bible, I did not really know how to accept Ham seeing the nakedness of Noah. The one thing that I did know is that Noah's nakedness was seen and that Noah was drunk. With the perversion of our current social society being so prevalent, my mind had no choice but to think of Noah's nakedness in a twisted manner. The situation was so grievous in the sight of God that a man and all his lineage became cursed. Of all that I heard of Noah's nakedness from the many religious leaders, I somewhat believed those varying views. But many of my questions still went unanswered. The more I read the Bible, the more my questions began to be answered by God's word. And because I was called to teach the word of God, the nakedness of Noah hit closer to home more than I could have ever imagined.

* * *

Noah was a man born before the great flood documented in Genesis. The word of God says that Noah was a preacher of righteousness (2 Pet. 2:4-5) and that "**. . . Noah found grace in the eyes of the LORD** [Gen. 6:8]." Noah was the first son of Lamech, and the grandson of Methuselah. When Noah was born, it was said of him, "**This *same* shall comfort us concerning our work and toil of our hands, because of the ground which the LORD hath cursed** [Gen. 5:29]."

Within the generation of Noah, the earth was corrupt before God. But Noah was the apple of God's eye. The scripture says that "**. . . Noah was a just man *and* perfect in his generations, *and* Noah walked with God** [Gen. 6:9]." During Noah's era, God declared that he would destroy all mankind from the face of the earth. Therefore, Noah was commanded by God to build an ark. God also spoke to Noah, saying, "**And, behold, I, even I, do bring a flood of waters upon the earth, to destroy all flesh, wherein *is* the breath of life, from under heaven; *and* everything that *is* in the earth shall die. But with thee will I establish my covenant; and thou shalt come into the ark, thou, and thy sons, and thy wife, and thy sons' wives with thee. And of every living thing of all flesh, two of every *sort* shalt thou bring into the ark, to keep *them* alive with thee; they shall be male and female** [Gen. 6:17-19]."

God adored Noah and trusted him with not only the survival of mankind but also the survival of the animal kingdom. There is nothing documented or written about the specific will of God for this particular generation, nor is there a detailed doctrine that would give us a sense of the perversion of man that grieved God so. But what we do have is a clear picture of the displeasure of God that prompted him to destroy almost everything that lived on land.

After building the ark as commanded by God, Noah was then told to enter the ark with all his family. It was time for God's judgment. When Noah was six hundred years old, the scripture says, "**. . . in the second month, the seventeenth day of the month, the same day were all the fountains of the great deep broken up, and the windows of heaven**(the sky) **were opened** [Gen. 7:11]." The floods came and covered the face of the whole earth, killing all that dwelled on the land. Only Noah and his family survived, along with all the animals that God had commanded Noah to place within the ark before the flood.

Once the waters began to dry up, Noah and his family stepped out of the ark into a whole new world where they were the torchbearers responsible for the growth of the human population from this time forward. We cannot imagine what crossed their minds as the reality of what just happened settled into their thoughts. The fear of God might have been the only thing dominant in their lives at this moment. To be wicked before God is an abomination, and to neglect God's will is an act of self-destruction. This had to be known. This had to be expressed. Everyone among the few survivors perhaps held question marks on their faces, constantly seeking the will of God for the sake of remaining obedient and escaping the fate that almost all of humanity had received.

Once things settled down, and the earth began to be overspread by the three sons of Noah, Noah resumed his duty as a preacher of righteousness. Noah began to comfort the people. Noah began to be a husbandman, and he planted a vineyard. This was within Noah's nature from birth. Noah was a natural born leader. Comforting others concerning the state of mankind was Noah's destiny, as declared at his birth. In due time Noah lowered his guard and became slack in his efforts. For this reason, the word reveals that ". . . **he drank of the wine** (of his vineyard), **and was drunken; and he was uncovered within his tent. And Ham, the father of Canaan, saw the nakedness of his father**(Noah), **and told his two brethren without**(outside) [Gen. 9:21-22]." What exactly did Ham see? And what does the nakedness of Noah truly represent? Glory be to God and his manifold wisdom; we will now recognize the error of Noah, the transgression of Noah's son Ham, and the compassion of Noah's two sons, Shem and Japheth.

* * *

The first thing that we must understand is that Noah planted a vineyard. This vineyard should not be interpreted as literal vines that produce grapes and berries for wine. The vineyard that Noah planted was people. Noah's wife, his three sons, and their wives, and the offspring that was eventually produced by Noah's sons became those who Noah would comfort concerning the state of mankind on earth. Therefore, after the flood, Noah moved forward within his calling as a preacher of righteousness, and a congregation(vineyard) was gathered unto him to continually hear Noah speak the will of God.

People are described as vineyards all throughout the Bible. Authors of the Old and New Testament spoke the parabolic language that compared collective groups of people to vineyards. The prophet Isaiah was a man of many words. As Isaiah spoke a prophetic parable concerning the wickedness of the children of Israel, Isaiah makes it plain to understand that he is not speaking of literal vines. Relaying the message of God, Isaiah says, "**NOW will I**(God) **sing to my**(his) **wellbeloved**(the children of Israel) **a song of my beloved touching his**(the children of Israel's) **vineyard**(people). **My wellbeloved hath a vineyard**(nation) **in a very fruitful hill** (the land of Canaan)**: And he**(God) **fenced it, and gathered out the stones**(Gentiles) **thereof, and planted it with the choicest**(Israelite) **vine, and built a tower**(priesthood) **in the mist of it, and also made a winepress**(temple) **therein: and he**(God) **looked that it**(the inhabitants of Judah) **should bring forth grapes, and it brought forth wild grapes. And now, O inhabitants of Jerusalem, and men of Judah, judge, I pray you, betwixt**(between) **me and my vineyard. What could have been done more to my vineyard, that I have not done in it? wherefore, when I looked that it should bring forth grapes, brought it forth wild grapes? And now go to; I will tell you what I will do to my vineyard: I will take away the hedge thereof, and it shall be eaten up;** *and* **break down the wall thereof, and it shall be trodden down: And I will lay it waste: it shall not be pruned, nor digged; but there shall come up briers and thorns: I will also command the clouds that they rain no rain upon it. For the vineyard of the LORD of host** *is* **the house of Israel, and the men of Judah his pleasant plant: and he looked for judgment, but behold oppression;** (God looked) **for righteousness, but behold a cry** [Isa. 5:1-7]."

The prophets of the Old Testament understood that the wisdom of God did not exist in the literal sense of all that they spoke. Many of their words were sometimes spoken indirectly, guiding our thoughts toward the spiritual characteristics of the symbols and attributes of the things they portrayed as they spoke. Jesus Christ was also familiar with the divine language that spoke of vineyards in the manner of a particular group of people. While in the temple of Jerusalem only days before he was crucified, Jesus used the words of the prophet Isaiah in a parable, seeking to show the Jews that they were rejecting their Savior and that they would pay a devastating price for doing so (Mat. 21:33-40). Jesus Christ ended the parable with this question to the Jews, saying, "**When the lord therefore of the vineyard cometh, what will he do unto those husbandmen**(leaders) [Mat. 21:40]?" And aside from the words of the prophet Isaiah, Jesus Christ spoke his very own parable using the word vineyard. In Matthew 20:1, Jesus Christ began a parable by saying, "**FOR the kingdom of heaven is like unto a man *that is* an householder, which went out early in the morning to hire labourers into his vineyard.**" Once we read this parable in its entirety, we will recognize that Jesus Christ is not speaking about literal vineyards that produce berries and grapes.

Furthermore, within the New Testament, the Apostle Paul also gave the example of planting a vineyard. The believers of the church in Corinth were Paul's particular vineyard for that city. The city of Corinth held a rambunctious set of believers. Or shall I say, there was a rambunctious sect of make-believers among the faithful believers within the Corinthian church? With the church of Corinth being founded by Paul, Paul was accepted as their leader in the form of the messenger of Christ. But in due time, some of those who acknowledged the testimony of Jesus Christ began to question Paul's authority, looking to proclaim their own versions of the gospel. The first letter to the Corinthians was Paul's response to those who needed to see that they were in error as they proclaimed to follow Jesus Christ.

When Paul defined his God-given authority as an apostle to the Corinthians, he wrote to those of the Corinthian church who opposed him, saying, "**AM I not an apostle? am I not free? have I not seen**

Jesus Christ our Lord? are not ye my work in the Lord? If I be not an apostle unto others, yet doubtless I am to you: for the seal of mine apostleship are ye in the Lord. Mine answer to them that do examine me is this, Have we not power(freedom) **to eat and to drink? Have we not power to lead about a sister, a wife, as well as other apostles, and *as* the brethren of the Lord, and Cephas**(Peter)**? Or I only and Barnabas, have not we power to forebear working? Who goeth a warfare anytime at his own charges? who planteth a vineyard**(congregation)**, and eateth not of the fruit thereof? or who feedeth a flock**(congregation)**, and eateth not of the milk of the flock** [1 Cor. 9:1-7]?"

Although Paul established many churches throughout the Roman Empire, his stay among them at the most would only last a few days, months, or years. He went from region to region and from city to city setting up churches and ordaining local Christian elders to head each church. Paul did not settle down and become the pastor of any particular church himself, as did Peter(Cephas) in the case of the Christian church in Jerusalem (Gal. 2:8-9). When Paul was among the believers in any city or region, he stayed focused on one thing: satisfying the will of God above all else. Of all the churches that Paul founded, he never became exclusively obligated to a certain church. He would immediately find able men, apt to teach, and place them in charge of the believers as he monitored them in various ways from time to time.

Paul did not attempt to lean towards the will of those congregations by indulging in their self-based agendas. Paul was there to lead, and lead is exactly what he did. The desires of a multitude will most always be backed by some form of selfish ideology. Therefore, those who are called to minister within the body of Christ must stay firm and not allow themselves to be taken advantage of through the influences of their congregations. As we can see, Paul planted many vineyards(churches) and did not eat of their fruit. Some of us may interpret these few words as an attempt by Paul to show that he did not receive material benefits from the congregation as their leader. More accurately, Paul was attempting to relay the message of faithfulness in the gospel by not accepting any self-satisfying desires of any congregation, regardless of the things that his followers might desire of him as they attempted to persuade him in one way or another.

Order within the body of Christ is one of the central themes of Paul's first letter to the Corinthians (1 Cor. 11:34/14:40). As Paul reintroduced himself to the Corinthians through his first letter to them, he wanted to express his faithfulness to the truth of the gospel. Paul was firm as he wrote to the Corinthians, saying, "**For it hath been declared unto me of you, my brethren, by them *which are of the house(church)* of Chloe, that there are contentions**(debating) **among you. Now this I say, that every one of you saith, I am of Paul; and I of Apollos; and I of Cephas**(Peter)**; and I of Christ. Is Christ divided? Was Paul crucified for you? or were you baptized in the name of Paul? I thank God that I baptized none of you, but Crispus and Gaius; Lest any should say that I had baptized in my own name** [1 Cor. 1:11-15]." Paul did not become drunk and naked by accepting the fact that the congregation that he planted was attempting to make their own choices of which minister to claim allegiance to in the gospel. Regardless of the minister, the pastor, or the teacher who introduces us to the gospel of Christ, in the New Covenant, there is only one choice of who to follow, Jesus Christ. Although Paul planted the vineyard of Corinth, Paul was not going to fall short and drink of the wine of his vineyard as did Noah.

Context is very important. Within the context of the words of Isaiah, Jesus Christ, and the Apostle Paul, we can see that metaphorically speaking, the word "vineyard" represents a collective group of people according to many situations within the Bible. Now that we have seen that the word "vineyard" is used to convey the image of a collective group of individuals formed by the leadership of someone, whether it be of God or man, we can now understand the nakedness of Noah more clearly. Noah's problem was not that he was leading his vineyard astray, so much as Noah's vineyard was leading him astray.

It is said that Noah drank of the wine of the vineyard that he planted. Therefore, with Noah accepting the desires of his congregation, he was led astray from manifesting the truth of God's will, thus becoming drunk. Within his drunkenness, Noah was not in a sound mind to display the true example of the will of God while continuing to lead the people; thus, Noah was uncovered according to the grace of God's righteousness abiding upon him.

* * *

In hearing the word "nakedness," we would automatically think of some form of nudity. To be fair to the reader, the word that is used to describe nakedness can also be defined as "shame" or "improper behavior." With Noah being uncovered within his tent(tabernacle), we must be aware that the word "uncovered" can also be defined as "to reveal himself." "Nakedness" and "uncovered" are words that combine to reflect an act of shamefulness. Noah's nakedness reflected his behavior, not his display of physical nudity.

Moreover, with the scripture saying that Ham saw the nakedness of his father, it must be noted that within other situations, the saying of "the nakedness of thy father" is also directed toward the wife of someone's father. The book of Leviticus makes this clear. Speaking of the immorality of incest among family members, the book of Leviticus states, "**None of you shall approach to any that is near kin to him, to uncover *their* nakedness: I *am* the LORD. The nakedness of thy father, or the nakedness of thy mother, shalt thou not uncover: she *is* thy mother; thou shalt not uncover her nakedness. The nakedness of thy father's wife shalt thou not uncover: it *is* thy father's nakedness** [Lev. 18:6-8]."

By using the scriptures of the book of Leviticus, some conclude that Noah's son Ham engaged in some form of sexual relations with either Noah or Noah's wife, thus uncovering Noah's nakedness. The scripture of Genesis 9:21 states that Noah was uncovered because of Noah's drunkenness, not because of a sexual relationship shared between Noah and his son Ham or Ham and Noah's wife.

As we seek for context in all that we read, it must be revealed that in almost every other place within the Old Testament that the nakedness of one's father appears, it is in reference to someone sharing a sexual relationship of some kind with his father's wife (Lev. 20:11

/ Eze. 22:10). In the case of Noah's nakedness alone, the context of the surrounding verses does not suggest a sexual theme of any kind. Noah's nakedness is in the direction of shame and uncleanness due to Noah's drunkenness. Noah's wife is never mentioned or suggested in the scripture. Therefore, if one chooses to assume that Noah's son Ham indulged in a sexual act with either Noah or Noah's wife, thereby seeing his father's nakedness, feel free to do so. But consider this one thing, does the surrounding scriptures of Genesis chapter 9, which describe Noah's situation, support such an interpretation? No, not at all. Noah being uncovered and Noah's nakedness are most definitely in the context of shamefulness due to Noah's error in drinking of the wine of his vineyard and becoming drunk. This is to say, Noah was influenced by the desires of the people(vineyard) and became misguided.

Furthermore, if Noah's nakedness is in reference to his son Ham sharing a sexual act with either Noah or Noah's wife, how then could Shem and Japheth, Noah's other two sons, cover Noah's nakedness? In the context of the events that take place in Genesis 9:18-27, if Noah's nakedness is in reference to Noah or his wife, there would be no covering up the act of adultery and incest. This could not have been accomplished by Shem and Japheth walking backward with a garment on both their shoulders and placing it over either Noah or Noah's wife. If so, we would have to acknowledge that Shem and Japheth did a poor job of attempting to cover up the sexual act that had taken place. Why do I say this? Because when Noah woke up from his drunkenness, Noah realized what had transpired. Noah's nakedness had nothing to do with his wife's infidelity.

By becoming drunk through the influence of his vineyard(congregation), Noah removed himself from under the covering of God's graceful guidance. Within Noah's perverted state of mind, his son Ham became aware that Noah was not in accordance with the will of God in the way he was leading the people. Once Ham understood that Noah was negligent, instead of explaining to his father that he was behaving contrary to God's will, Ham condoned Noah's behavior and let it be. Ham then went out and told his two brothers, Shem and Japheth, of their father's state.

Noah was indeed naked, and the New Testament authors also help to reveal the heavenly interpretation of the nakedness that Noah experienced. When speaking of those who were blind to their own nakedness, it is said within the book of Revelation, "**Because thou sayest, I am rich, and increased with goods, and have need of nothing; and knowest not that thou art wretched, and miserable, and poor, and blind, and naked: I counsel thee to buy of me gold tried in the fire, that thou mayest be rich; and white raiment, that thou mayest be clothed, and *that* the shame of thy nakedness do not appear; and anoint thine eyes with eyesalve, that thou mayest see** [Rev. 3:17-18]." Noah was not aware of his nakedness. He needed someone to anoint his eyes with eye salve so that he could realize the state he was in. Although the scriptures of Revelation are speaking in terms of the New Testament era, the situation of Noah's nakedness is a great example of what the scriptures of Revelation 3:17-18 are referring to.

* * *

The flood that destroyed almost all human kind was still fresh in the memories of Shem and Japheth. The flood was an event that they experienced because of man's disobedience in the sight of God. The way in which the scriptures read, upon hearing the words of Ham, Shem, and Japheth, immediately set out to correct the situation before any more damage could be done. It is apparent that Shem and Japheth responded with action. The scripture says, "**And Shem and Japheth took a garment, and laid *it* upon both their shoulders, and went backward, and covered the nakedness of their father; and their faces *were* backward, and they saw not their father's nakedness** [Gen. 9:23]."

Shem and Japheth took a garment, laid it on both their shoulders, went backward, and covered the nakedness of their father, Noah. Is this to say that Shem and Japheth literally walked backward with a sheet or a blanket on both their shoulders in order to cover up the incest that had taken place between Noah and his son Ham or between Ham and

Noah's wife? I think not! The garment that Shem and Japheth placed on both their shoulders is a metaphorical symbol of the responsibility that they accepted in order to correct the mistake that had come about through Noah's drunkenness. The word "garment" is often used within the Bible to represent a unique form of divine righteousness, while at other times, it represents man's self-righteousness.

Although the book of Genesis is the first book of the Bible, the revelation of its contents was given to Moses by God. The first eleven chapters of the book of Genesis hold some of the most metaphorical passages contained within the entire Bible. Metaphors and parables are nothing new when we think of the Prophets of the Old Testament or even the New Testament messengers of the gospel. Despite this, many would exclude the book of Genesis when thinking of metaphors or even parables.

Moving forward many generations from Noah, we can see that Jesus Christ also used the word "garment" to create the image of a justifiable spirit in a parable. During the last year of his ministry, while in the temple in Jerusalem, Jesus spoke of the kingdom of God in a parable, saying, "**The kingdom of heaven is like unto a certain king, which made a marriage for his son, And sent forth his servants to call them that were bidden to the wedding: and they would not come** [Mat. 22.2-3]."

According to the true interpretation of the parable, after the Jews who were invited to the wedding refused to come, the king sent his servants out into the highways to invite as many Gentiles as would come to his son's wedding. Once the wedding was furnished with all the "invited" guests, the king came to see them. The king immediately noticed that something was wrong. Someone had shown up to the wedding uninvited. The scripture says, "**And when the king came in to see the guests, he saw there a man which had not on a wedding garment: And he saith unto him, Friend, how camest thou in hither**(here) **not having a wedding garment? And he**(the uninvited guest) **was speechless. Then said the king to the servants, Bind him**(the uninvited guest) **hand and foot, and take him away, and cast *him* into outer darkness; there shall be weeping and gnashing of teeth. For many are called, but few** *are* **chosen** [Mat. 22:11-14]." The uninvited guest showed up to the wedding, not having the proper spirit to attend. A spirit that is willing to accept God's will and become obedient to the example of Jesus Christ is the garment that God would have approved as the proper wedding attire.

Furthermore, within the book of Revelation, the word "garment" is also used as a form of righteousness. When the Lord spoke to the angel of the church in Sardis, he said, "**Thou hast a few names even in Sardis which have not defiled their garments; and they shall walk with me in white: for they are worthy** [Rev. 3:4]." And once again, as John spoke of the wrath of God within chapter 16 of the book of Revelation, the scripture says, "**Behold, I come as a thief. Blessed *is* he that watcheth, and keepeth his garments, lest he walk naked, and they see his shame** [Rev. 16:15]." The garments that are spoken of within the book of Revelation reveal that the word garment is also used to convey an image of spiritual righteousness.

* * *

With the scripture saying that Shem and Japheth placed the garment on both their shoulders, this portrays the image of the spiritual integrity that Shem and Japheth held within their hearts. It also indicates that they both were willing to take the burden of correcting their father's shamefulness on themselves. Putting things on our shoulders is a symbol of our attempt to bear it. In fact, after God removed the Israelites out of Egypt, certain family members of the tribe of Levi were commanded to bear the ark of the covenant on their shoulders as an image of the burden of their priesthood (Num. 7:9).

Even when it came to a prophecy concerning Jesus Christ, Isaiah used the word "shoulder." As Isaiah spoke of the responsibilities of the coming Messiah, he said, "**For unto us a child is born, unto us a son is given: and the government shall be upon his shoulder: and his name shall be called Wonderful, Counsellor, The mighty God, The everlasting Father, The Prince of Peace** [Isa. 9:6]." I know that we are not naive enough to think that Jesus Christ walked around with the principles of the NEW Testament literally bound on his shoulder. Setting the standard of righteousness, which would invite eternal life into the souls of all that believe in him, would become Christ's burden to carry all alone. Jesus Christ carried this burden in his heart. That which was in Christ's heart was shown openly through the things which Christ achieved. Christ's shoulder represents the burden of his heart. Christ's shoulder also represents the responsibilities that he accepted in his heart as he stepped forward to sacrifice his time, his effort, and his life for the sake of the gospel.

Furthermore, Paul showed within his letter to the Galatians how he had to form the righteousness of Christ in the hearts of the Galatians once again (Gal. 4:19-20) after they were led astray by those who were perverting the truth of the gospel (Gal. 1:6-7). Through his own words, Paul expressed a present-day example of the situation that exemplifies bearing one another's burdens, saying, "**BRETHREN** (of Galatia)**, if a man be overtaken in a fault, ye which are spiritual, restore such an one in the spirit of meekness; considering thyself, lest thou also be tempted. Bear ye one another's burdens, and so fulfill the law of Christ** [Gal. 6:1-2]." Although Noah and his family were living in a different era than that of the Galatians, the same example of bearing one another's burdens in the spirit of meekness corresponds with the actions of Shem and Japheth.

* * *

Noah's sons Shem and Japheth went backward, which is to say that Shem and Japheth turned to the will of God in order to correct the situation, thereby restoring their father back into the leader that he once was rather than the follower that he had become. The scripture says that Shem and Japheth's ". . . faces *were* backward. . . ." This portion of the scripture represents the pureness of Shem and Japheth's intentions. The clear image of Shem and Japheth's characters shows that they did not care about the previous things done by their father because they were not there to see nor indulge in the error of Noah's drunkenness. Shem and Japheth's efforts were motivated by their willingness to retrace the steps that led their father astray and correct Noah's error, thus going backward and covering Noah's nakedness.

After Shem and Japheth revealed to Noah his nakedness(uncleanness) and his drunkenness(error), Noah accepted the efforts of his two sons as they went about correcting Noah's folly. The covering of one another's nakedness is welcoming in the sight of God. The famous and wise king Solomon wrote in the book of Proverbs that "**Hatred stirreth up strifes: but love covereth all sins** [Pro. 10:12]." And James, the brother of Jesus Christ, followed Solomon's lead by writing in his general epistle, saying, "**Brethren, if any of you do err from the truth, and one convert him; Let him know, that he which converteth the sinner from the error of his way, shall save a soul from death, and shall hide**(cover) **a multitude of sins** [Jam. 5:19-20]."

* * *

With the error of Noah now being revealed to him by Shem and Japheth, Noah recognized his faults and acknowledged that they had delivered him from his state of drunkenness. Noah also realized something else. Soon afterward, Noah apparently grew angry with his son Ham. The scripture reveals, "**And Noah awoke from his wine**(drunkenness), **and knew what his younger son** (Ham) **had done unto him. And he said, Cursed** *be* **Canaan; a servant of servants shall he be unto his brethren. And he**(Noah) **said, Blessed** *be* **the LORD God of Shem; and Canaan shall be his servant. God shall enlarge Japheth, and he shall dwell in the tents of Shem; and Canaan shall be his servant** [Gen. 9:24-27]."

Noah drank of the wine of his vineyard and became drunk. This is to say, Noah began to serve the people more than God. Instead of remaining faithful in his leadership as a preacher of righteousness, Noah caved to the influences of his congregation and unconsciously became the follower. Noah began to lean towards the will of the people above the will of God, thereby becoming drunk, unstable, and behaving shamefully according to God's righteousness. Noah's son Ham recognized this, but instead of informing Noah of his error, Ham went from the presence of Noah and told Shem and Japheth of the matter. Shem and Japheth immediately approached their father to correct the matter at hand. Noah recognized his error through the efforts of Shem and Japheth, then Noah cursed his grandson Canaan, the son of Ham.

Ham had seen his father's error and failed to sincerely care for his father's state. Shem and Japheth, on the other hand, moved with urgency and compassion and sought to immediately correct Noah's drunkenness by revealing to Noah that he was out of order in the manner that he was leading. As Noah awoke to his shortcoming, he also realized that his son Ham had shown disrespect to the law of God by consciously and intentionally allowing him to continue forward in his error and by revealing Noah's error to others without first attempting to reveal Noah's error to Noah himself.

* * *

The book of Genesis is the revelation of the beginning. Most of the events written therein are literal. However, there are certain situations that are written in a metaphorical dialect, preserving the wisdom of God and revealing the heavenly language to Christian generations that are ready to receive it. Moses simply proclaimed the message of God, but it is God who teaches us his hidden wisdom. Noah's nakedness had nothing to do with homosexuality or incest. Neither did Noah's nakedness have anything to do with sexual intercourse between Noah's wife and his son Ham.

There are examples of Noah's nakedness existing right now at this present time throughout the world. Many take on themselves the burden of covering the nakedness(shamefulness) of others through their efforts in the truth. And unfortunately, there are many others who look for opportunities to exploit the nakedness(shamefulness) of others through falsehood by taking advantage of their drunkenness. We should do all that we can to remain sober and clothed with the righteousness of God's word and not be found drunk and naked in his sight. The nakedness of Noah has just been revealed in Divine Context.

Context #4 reveals how Jacob wrestled with God in prayer because he was afraid to face his brother Esau alone.

GENESIS 32:24-25

24. And Jacob was left alone; and there wrestled a man with him until the breaking of the day.

25. And when he(the man) saw that he prevailed not against him(Jacob), he touched the hollow of his thigh; and the hollow of Jacob's thigh was out of joint, as he(the man) wrestled with him.

Jacob Wrestled With God

Divine Context is understanding that the man Jacob wrestled with was not a physical being, as of someone existing in the flesh. On the contrary, the man that wrestled with Jacob was the presence of God, revealing to Jacob that he would fight his battle for him.

* * *

This wresting match between God and Jacob was the result of Jacob's fear of facing his brother Esau as he returned home after being gone for two decades. Jacob is the son of Isaac and the grandson of Abraham. Abraham, Isaac, and Jacob were the three individuals that God had promised to bless with descendants as numerous as the stars above and as plentiful as the sand on the seashores (Gen. 15:1-5/26:1-5/28:10-15).

According to old-time customs, when a family began to have children, the first male child would be the one to inherit the largest portion of the family legacy, and he will often be the one to represent his family's name (Deu. 21:15-17). This happened when Isaac was born to Abraham. And Isaac looked forward to doing the same with his first-born child. Isaac made a request to the LORD for his wife Rebekah as he sought to begin his own family because, at this time,

Rebekah was unable to bear children. The LORD heard Isaac's prayer, and shortly thereafter, Rebekah became pregnant with twins. From within Rebekah's womb, a battle for supremacy began between the two children. As the children struggled within her womb, Rebekah cried out to God, saying, "**If** *it be* **so, why** *am* **I thus** [Gen. 25:22]?" Then the LORD said to Rebekah, "**Two nations** *are* **in thy womb, and two manner of people shall be separated from thy bowels; and** *the one* **people shall be stronger than** *the other* **people; and the elder shall serve the younger** [Gen. 25:23]."

When the time of her delivery arrived, she gave birth to twins, just as God had said. They named the first child Esau and the second child they named Jacob. According to tradition, because Esau was the first child to arrive, he should have inherited the birthright of the first-born. God, however, had other plans.

As the children grew older, Esau became a man of the field and a hunter. His brother Jacob, though, was a gentle man, dwelling in tents. On a certain day, Jacob prepared himself a meal as Esau came in from the field. Being faint, Esau begged for the food that his brother Jacob had just prepared. Esau's exact words to Jacob were, "**Feed me, I pray thee, with that same red** *pottage;* **for I** *am* **faint . . .** [Gen. 25:30]." Jacob responded to Esau's request, saying, "**Sell me this day thy birthright** [Gen. 25:31]." Esau did not care for his birthright and sold it to Jacob that very same day, despising all that was to come to him of his father's blessing (Gen. 25:34).

It came to pass that Isaac felt the day of his death was drawing near: therefore, he called his eldest son Esau to him, saying, "**Behold now, I am old, I know not the day of my death: Now therefore take, I pray thee, thy weapons, thy quiver**(arrows) **and thy bow, and go out to the field, and take me** *some* **venison**(deer)**: And make me savoury meat, such as I love, and bring** *it* **to me, that I may eat; that my soul may bless thee before I die** [Gen. 27:2-4]."

Although Isaac loved Esau above Jacob, Isaac's wife Rebekah loved Jacob above Esau (Gen. 25:28). Overhearing all that Isaac said to Esau, Rebekah went quickly and found Jacob. Rebekah then prepared a meal and dressed Jacob as if he were Esau and sent Jacob in to feed his father with anticipation of receiving the blessing of the firstborn. Following the instructions of his mother, Jacob brought the food to his father. Isaac's eyes were dim because of his old age; therefore, he could not discern that it was Jacob who provided him with the meal. As a result, Jacob received the blessing of the firstborn.

Soon after Jacob left the presence of his father, Esau came in. As Esau was about to offer his father the food that he went out to fetch, Isaac, in his surprise, said to Esau, "**Who *art* thou? . . . where *is* he that hath taken venison, and brought *it* me, and I have eaten of all before thou camest, and have blessed him? yea, *and* he shall be blessed** [Gen. 27:32-33]." Esau then realized that Jacob had stolen away his birthright, "**And Esau lifted up his voice, and wept** [Gen. 27:38]." Esau also received a blessing from his father Isaac, but in Esau's heart, the blessing that his father had given to him was second-rate in comparison to the blessing that Jacob received. Esau began to hate his brother and sought vengeance on him, saying in his heart, "**The days of mourning for my father are at hand; then will I slay my brother Jacob** [Gen. 27:41]."

Their mother, Rebekah, was told of the thoughts of Esau how he wanted to kill his own brother. She then asked Jacob to run away to a place called Haran and dwell there with her brother Laban until Esau's anger be turned away. Jacob listened to the words of his mother and departed from his homeland, the land of Canaan.

So, Jacob left his family behind and headed off into a strange land. As he traveled, he came to a certain place, and there he spent the night. When Jacob fell asleep, the LORD appeared to him in a dream and said, "**I *am* the LORD God of Abraham thy father, and the God of Isaac: the land whereon thou liest**(lay)**, to thee will I give it, and to thy seed; And thy seed shall be as the dust of the earth, and thou shalt spread abroad to the west, and to the east, and to the north, and to the south: and in thee and in thy seed shall all the families**(Gentiles) **of the earth be blessed. And, behold, I *am* with thee, and will keep thee in all *places* whither thou goest, and will bring thee again into this land; for I will not leave thee, until I have done *that* which I have spoken to thee of** [Gen. 28:13-15]."

Jacob called the name of the place where he had the dream Bethel.

Jacob then poured oil on the stones that he used for pillows and made a vow to the LORD, saying, "**If God will be with me, and will keep me in this way that I go, and will give me bread to eat, and raiment**(clothing) **to put on, So that I come again to my father's house in peace; then shall the LORD be my God: And this stone, which I have set *for* a pillar, shall be God's house: and of all that thou shalt give me I will surely give the tenth unto thee** [Gen. 28:20-22]."

Once Jacob came to the city of Haran, he began to work for his uncle Laban and married both of his daughters: Leah and Rachel. It came to pass that after twenty years of working for his uncle Laban; friction began to build between the two. Therefore, God said to Jacob, "**Return unto the land of thy fathers, and to thy kindred; and I will be with thee** [Gen. 31:3]."

Twenty years had passed, and eleven sons and one daughter were born to Jacob of his two wives and their maids in the land of Syria (Gen. 29:31-30:24). After the first fourteen years of working for his uncle Laban, Jacob now wanted his own; so, he made a proposition to care for Laban's livestock and thereby receive a portion for himself. Laban agreed to Jacob's proposal, and Jacob began to work towards building up his wealth in order to provide for his own family.

For the next six years, God blessed Jacob, and his livestock grew even larger than that of his uncle Laban's. Seeing this, Laban and his sons became hostile toward Jacob. God then appeared to Jacob in a dream. Understanding what his next step needed to be, Jacob called both his wives to him and said, "**I see your father's countenance, that it *is* not towards me as before; but the God of my father hath been with me. And ye know that with all my power I have served your father. And your father hath deceived me, and changed my wages ten times; but God suffered**(allowed) **him not to hurt me. Thus God hath taken away the cattle of your father, and given *them* to me. And the angel of God spake unto me in a dream, *saying,* Jacob: And I said, Here *am* I. And he**(God) **said, . . . I am the God of Bethel, where thou aniontedst the pillar, *and* where thou vowedst a vow unto me: now arise, get thee out from this land, and return unto the land of thy kindred** [Gen. 31:5-7,9,11-13]."

Jacob then gathered together all his goods, along with his entire family, and left Padanaram(Syria) immediately. Once Laban heard that Jacob had run off, he gathered his sons and pursued after Jacob. But when Laban caught up to Jacob in Gilead, God had already settled the matter showing himself to be on Jacob's side. Laban wanted to do harm to Jacob, but God would not allow him to do so. While in the presence of Jacob, Laban confessed his intentions, saying, "**It is in the power of my hand to do you hurt: but the God of your father spake unto me yesternight, saying, Take thou heed that thou speak not to Jacob either good or bad** [Gen. 31:29]." After Laban was given the opportunity to bid his daughters farewell, he and Jacob parted ways. As Jacob journeyed towards his homeland, all things seemed to be good.

* * *

Now that Jacob was back in the familiar country of his youth, there was one last thing that he needed to deal with. The thought of his brother Esau began to weigh heavily on his mind. So, Jacob sent his servants ahead of him to greet his brother before they would enter one another's presence once again. Twenty years earlier, Esau planned to kill Jacob because he accused Jacob of stealing his birthright.

In the time that had passed, God had shown Jacob great favor. Jacob's wealth had grown abundantly. Therefore, Jacob sent servants ahead with a gift to let Esau know that God had blessed him, hoping to find favor in Esau's sight. When Jacob's servants returned from offering Esau the gift, they said to Jacob, "**We came to thy brother Esau, and also he comest to meet thee, and four hundred men with him** [Gen. 32:6]."

This is where the wrestling match between God and Jacob begins. Upon hearing that Esau was on his way to meet him with four hundred men, Jacob was troubled; for the scripture says, "**Then Jacob was greatly afraid and distressed: and he divided the people that *was* with him, and the flocks, and the herds, and the camels, into two bands; And said, If Esau come to the one company, and smite(kill) it, then the other company which is left shall escape** [Gen. 32:7-8]."

Jacob was confused, afraid, and distressed. At this point, Jacob turned to God, seeking an answer from heaven. Sounds familiar, doesn't it? We have all been here. When all else fails, we know who to call on. Things did not look good for Jacob, and no doubt his thoughts returned to the death threat made by his brother Esau those many years ago. That same death threat was the main reason why Jacob departed from his homeland in the first place.

Nevertheless, Jacob did not panic, nor did he run the other way. Jacob did not prepare himself to do battle with his brother Esau by gathering all his servants together and arming them with weapons of war. Jacob took his argument to God, reminding God of why he was in this position, saying, "**O God of my father Abraham, and God of my father Isaac, the LORD which saidst unto me, Return unto thy country, and to thy kindred, and I will deal well with thee: I am not worthy of the least of all the mercies, and of all the truth, which thou hast shewed unto thy servant; for with my staff I passed over this Jordan; and now I am become two bands. Deliver me, I pray thee, from the hand of my brother, from the hand of Esau: for I fear him, lest he will come and smite(kill) me, *and* the mother with the children. And thou saidst, I will surely do thee good, and make thy seed as the sand of the sea, which cannot be numbered for multitude** [Gen. 32:9-12]."

The bell had rung, and this wrestling match between God and Jacob was already in progress. Jacob poured out his heart to God, reminding God of his own words to protect him and allow his seed to grow as numerous as the sand on the seashores. Yes, God said that he would protect Jacob twenty years ago, but right now, Esau was on his way with four hundred men. Once Jacob saw his brother Esau in person, there was no telling if Jacob would survive, let alone his seed. But God is someone to trust, so Jacob stayed the course even in his fear. Jacob separated many goats, rams, camels, bulls, asses(donkeys), and foals. Jacob then gave all these animals to his servants so that they could provide them as a present once again to his brother Esau.

Jacob feared his brother, so he took his family and hid from Esau, passing over the marsh. That night when Jacob was alone, the scripture says, "... there **wrestled a man** (God) **with him**(Jacob) **until the breaking of the day. And when he**(God) **saw that he prevailed not against him, he**(God) **touched the hollow**(tendon) **of his thigh: and the hollow of Jacob's thigh was out of joint, as he wrestled with him. And he**(God) **said, Let me go, for the day breaketh. And he**(Jacob) **said, I will not let thee go, except thou bless me. And he**(God) **said unto him, What** *is* **thy name? And he said, Jacob. And he**(God) **said, Thy name shall be called no more Jacob, but Israel: for as a prince hast thou power with God and with men, and hast prevailed. And Jacob asked** *him,* **and said, Tell** *me,* **I pray thee, thy name. And he said, Wherefore** *is* **it** *that* **thou dost ask after my name? And he**(God) **blessed him there. And Jacob called the name of the place Peniel: for I have seen God face to face, and my life is preserved. And as he passed over Penuel the sun rose upon him, and he halted**(limped) **upon his thigh. Therefore the children of Israel eat not** *of* **the sinew**(tendon) **which shrank, which** *is* **upon the hollow of the thigh, unto this day: because he**(God) **touched the hollow of Jacob's thigh in the sinew**(tendon) **that shrank** [Gen. 32:24-32]."

It was not that Jacob wrestled with God so much as that God wrestled with Jacob. Jacob's struggle only pertained to the words of God, which promised to protect Jacob, and for Jacob to return to the homeland of his kindred. After looking at all that was taking place this night, we should be able to recognize that Jacob was in prayer, wrestling with the words that God had previously spoken to him. Jacob was seeking an answer from God that would comfort his heart. In return, God wrestled with Jacob trying to assure him that everything would be alright. Jacob's comfort came in the form of the name Israel. The name Israel bears the meaning of "God strives," "God rules," "God heals," and "he(Jacob's enemies) strives against God."

Jacob stayed in prayer all night on his knees, seeking an answer from God. Before Jacob gave in to God's attempt to assure him that he would be safe, Jacob demanded a blessing that would satisfy his soul. Jacob prevailed against God in that he did not give up in prayer. Jacob's persistence paid off, and God finally granted Jacob his blessing. God gave Jacob the name of Israel, and it was now evident that God was going to fight Jacob's battles, rule the heavens on behalf of Jacob, and heal the wounds between Jacob and his brother Esau. If Esau wanted to fight, it was against God he would have to battle. Receiving this blessing from God, Jacob now accepted that God was on his side. God had intimately revealed himself to Jacob and had given Jacob the strength to believe that he would be safe.

The scripture says that a man wrestled with Jacob. That man was God. The wrestling occurred during prayer. God and Jacob were wrestling over the promises that God had previously spoken to Jacob. We all have experienced what Jacob was going through. If we were facing an uncertain situation and God spoke to us, saying that in an hour, things would be perfectly fine, if things did not look any better after forty-five minutes, a wrestling match would ensue. We would begin to cry out to God, reminding him of all that he had said to us. We would be looking forward to an answer from God that would settle our thoughts.

It does not have to be a matter of life and death for us to begin to wrestle with God for a pleasing outcome within an uncertain situation. From trying to get a job to holding a loving relationship together through difficult times to even struggling with life's many temptations, most of us wrestle with the will of God from time to time.

* * *

We can confirm that the wrestling match between God and Jacob occurred during prayer rather than during a physical altercation because the prophet Hosea revisits the event that took place between Jacob and God that night. God called Hosea to be a prophet over a thousand years after his wresting match with Jacob. Hosea's ministry took place during the time of the kingdoms of Israel and Judah. The people of Israel had become divided into two separate kingdoms, and they all were mired deep in idolatry. As the prophet Hosea spoke of the whoredom(idolatry) of the two kingdoms, Hosea also reminded the Israelites that all the things that the LORD had done for them should be remembered, saying, "**The LORD hath also a controversy with Judah, and will punish Jacob**(the Israelites) **according to his ways;**

according to his doings will he(God) **recompense him. He took his brother by the heel in the womb, and by his strength he had power with God: Yea, he had power over the angel**(messenger)**, and prevailed: he wept, and made supplication**(prayer) **unto him**(God)**: he found him**(God) *in* **Bethel, and there he spake with us; Even the LORD God of host; the LORD** *is* **his memorial. Therefore turn thou to thy God: keep mercy and judgment, and wait on thy God continually** [Hos. 12:2-6]."

Those who are saved and those who are not saved; those who believe in the word of God and those who do not believe in the word of God; those who read the Bible religiously and those who read the Bible leisurely; no matter who we are, what country we are from, or how rich our cultural backgrounds may be, many of us will initially look at Jacob's experience as if he wrestled with a physical being. According to the Biblical language, an "angel" is simply defined as a messenger of God, which may appear in a variety of forms in order to reveal the purposed will of God towards mankind. The angel of God, in this case, was God's very own words. Jacob wrestled with the same words that God used to speak to Jacob in Bethel, saying, "**And, behold, I** *am* **with thee, and will keep thee in all** *places* **whither thou goest, and will bring thee again into this land; for I will not leave thee, until I have done** *that* **which I have spoken to thee of** [Gen. 28:15]." And Jacob was also wrestling with the same words that God used to speak to him in Haran twenty years later, saying, "**I** *am* **the God of Bethel, where thou anointedst the pillar,** *and* **where thou vowedst a vow unto me: now arise, get thee out from this land, and return unto the land of thy kindred** [Gen. 31:13]."

Saint John also defined the unity of God and God's word in the first verse of his declaration of the gospel of Jesus Christ, saying, "**IN the beginning was the Word, and the Word was with God, and the Word was God** [John 1:1]." When we wrestle with the words that God has spoken to us, we then enter a direct wrestling match with God. Whether God speaks to us through a man of God, a woman of God, or even directly, the words of God that are being spoken are the representation of God. The word of God is what inspires us, what motivates us, and what encourages us. The word of God is also that which chastises and condemns us. But when we become fearful of the things taking place around us, what and who do we seek in order to receive comfort when all else fails? We seek God's word, thereby seeking God. God's word (Holy Bible) is the reminder and the messenger that we constantly seek when we are in extremely uncertain situations.

When Jacob's grandfather Abraham separated himself from his cousin Lot, what came to Abraham in a vision? Was it God? Yes. Was it a messenger of God? Yes. Was it the presence of God? Once again, yes! The scripture says that it was the word of God that appeared to Abraham in a vision, saying, "**Fear not, Abram: I *am* thy shield, *and thy exceeding great reward*** [Gen. 15:1]." The word of God itself is the authoritative life form that we wrestle with during fearful situations. The fact that the prophet Hosea said that Jacob made supplication reveals that Jacob was in prayer, wrestling with the message that God had given him to return to the land of his kindred. One could then ask, "What about the hollow of Jacob's thigh that it was out of joint as God wrestled with him?" The scripture certainly says that Jacob halted upon his thigh because of the sinew of his thigh that shrank.

The sinew of Jacob's thigh is the tendons and the ligaments that are joined from one bone to another, helping to hold together and stabilize the skeletal frame. The hollow of Jacob's tendon is what shrank. The hollow is the center portion of the tendon that is not attached to either bone. A great example of this is when we take a large rubber band and stretch it in opposite directions. The width of its center (which would be the hollow part because it is not bound in either hand) will shrink inwardly because the tension is now being placed at both ends.

Now imagine that the rubber band is the tendon of our hips and thighs being expanded during a long night of prayer. The center portion of the tendon would shrink just as the center portion of the rubber band did. Do you think that we would be able to hop right up from a long night of prayer and walk away without limping? I think not. The tendons that connect Jacob's thigh bone to his hip bone were stretched due to the prostrated position that Jacob held as he prayed to God all that night.

The gristle, the tendon, the sinew, or the joint, however we want to say it, is what became sacred to the children of Israel because it symbolized the efforts of Jacob as he wrestled with God concerning his survival. Jacob undoubtedly limped away from the scene after battling God for a comforting answer in prayer all that night.

* * *

The man that wrestled with Jacob was God. To say that God is a man is not subject to Jacob's situation alone. In the book of Exodus, God allowed the children of Israel to pass through the Red Sea on dry land, and when the Egyptians attempted to follow them, they all drowned. Within the song that the children of Israel dedicated to God for helping them escape from Pharaoh and the Egyptians, the people said that "**The LORD *is* a man of war: the LORD *is* his name** [Exo. 15:3]." When certain individuals within the scriptures say that God is a man, it should never be taken literally as in fleshly terms. When the prophet Samuel revealed to king Saul that God had taken away the kingdom from him, Samuel then said to Saul, "**And also the Strength of Israel will not lie nor repent: for he *is* not a man, that he should repent** [1 Sam. 15:29]." Also, Jesus Christ confessed to the woman at the well in a city of Samaria called Sychar that "**God *is* a Spirit: and they that worship him**(God) **must worship *him***(*God*) **in spirit and in truth** [John 4:24]." Within Jacob's situation, the word "man" merely shows that God is intimately aware of our state. The spirits that inhabit our fleshly bodies were made in the image of God. Our fleshly body itself was formed out of the clay(dust) of the ground. Just as God is spirit, we are also spirit. Unfortunately, unlike God, our spirits are subject to infirmities to a certain degree because of the fleshly form that holds our spirits in bondage.

God wrestled with Jacob trying to persuade him that he would fight his battles. In return, Jacob wrestled with the word(messenger) of God that told him to return to his homeland. Jacob had stayed the course through much uncertainty, and now in his fear, Jacob sought a blessing that would comfort his heart. Jacob passed the test, and now he was learning the lesson. Over many years, God had allowed Jacob to survive the hostility of his father-in-law Laban, and now God was ready to show Jacob that the turmoil between him and his brother Esau was already over. Remaining in prayer all that night and demanding a blessing from God, Jacob's endurance led God to reveal to him that he had prevailed in his struggle with God and with man. The next step for Jacob was to experience the manifestation of God's word coming to pass before his own eyes.

When Esau received Jacob with open arms the next morning, Jacob was relieved and begged for his brother Esau to accept the gift he offered, saying, "**. . . I pray thee, if now I have found grace in thy sight, then receive my present at my hand: for therefore I have seen thy face, as though I had seen the face of God, and thou wast pleased with me** [Gen. 33:10]." The graciousness that Esau showed Jacob the next morning was the result of the wrestling match that had taken place between Jacob and God. The face of God was the truth of God's word coming to pass before Jacob's very own eyes.

* * *

Many of us have turned this sacred event between Jacob and God into something other than an intimate prayer session. There are some who have even produced drawings of Jacob in a physical wrestling match with a supposed angel. These images reflect the ways and the imaginations of man. These images remove the heavenly context of the situation and place it into a realm of science fiction. Whether we are familiar with the situation concerning the wrestling match between God and Jacob or not, when we read about it, we often concentrate on the wrestling match itself while ignoring why the wrestling match between God and Jacob occurred in the first place. The context of each verse does not exist within the verse itself. The context of each verse written within the Bible, each event documented within the Bible, and each situation preserved within the Bible is identified through everything that inspired it, provoked it, and produced it.

As we struggle with God's will day by day, we can be assured that our sincerity will give us the strength to prevail. As we grapple with the many questions, we can believe that God knows best and that God will help us overcome the fearful situations that life often brings our way. And as we wrestle with God from time to time, we can look to Jacob's persistence in prayer and gain comfort, believing that God is present in the battle. The wrestling match that took place between God and Jacob has just been revealed in Divine Context.

Context #5 reveals that the two greatest commandments are not a part of the original Ten Commandments and why the two greatest commandments were spoken forty years apart from one another.

DEUTERONOMY 6:4-5

4. Hear, O Israel: The LORD our God *is* one LORD.
5. And thou shalt love the LORD thy God with all thine heart, and with all thy soul, and with all thy might.

LEVITICTUS 19:18

18. Thou shalt not avenge, nor bear any grudge against the children of thy people, but thou shalt love thy neighbour as thyself: I *am* the LORD.

The Two Greatest Commandments

Divine Context is understanding that when God declared the Ten Commandments to the children of Israel on Mount Horeb, the two greatest commandments were not included within those ten commandments.

* * *

There were many different commandments written within the Old Testament that came to an end once Jesus Christ completed his ministry by dying on the cross and rising from the dead three days later. The principles of the Old Testament law were mainly based on the sacrifices of animals and the shedding of animal blood to make an atonement for the sins of the people (Lev. 17:10-11). Jesus Christ became the ultimate sacrifice when he allowed his blood to be shed, becoming the human sacrifice that would make an atonement for the sin of all those who believe in his righteousness (Heb. 9:13-14).

Before Jesus Christ was crucified on the cross, he declared two commandments to be the greatest commandments of all. When Jesus was in the temple in the city of Jerusalem, he taught many of the people about the kingdom of God. As Jesus taught, there were members of several Jewish religious groups present. They who opposed Jesus were the Herodians, the Sadducees, and the Pharisees (Mat. 22:15-16,34). They were all religious groups of the Jews, who confessed their belief in God and their devotion to the law of Moses, but each sect held its own opinion of how to interpret the law of Moses. These groups began to say things to Jesus, trying to upset him so they could accuse him of saying something against the Jewish law.

Throughout the years, these religious organizations of the Jews had directed much of their attention to the commandments of the law of Moses that focused on the carnal sacrifices rather than the commandments of the law that focused on spiritual obedience (Mat. 23:23-28). As Jesus Christ preached to the people who were in the temple, the Sadducees began to question Jesus concerning the resurrection of the dead. Once Jesus Christ put the Sadducees to shame by the answer that he gave them, a lawyer of the Pharisees then came looking to determine if Jesus was as wise as he seemed. Therefore, the lawyer said to Jesus, "**Master, which *is* the great commandment in the law** [Mat. 22:36]?" Jesus then answered the lawyer, saying, "**The first of all the commandments *is*, Hear, O Israel; The Lord our God is one Lord: And thou shalt love the Lord thy God with all thy heart, and with all thy soul, and with all thy mind, and with all thy strength: this *is* the first commandment. And the second *is* like, *namely* this, Thou shalt love thy neighbour as thyself. There is none other commandment greater than these** [Mark 12:29-31]." And with these words, the religious leaders acknowledged that they were not prepared to oppose Jesus at this time.

* * *

Approximately fifteen hundred years before Jesus Christ declared two commandments to be greater than all the other commandments, the children of Israel were held in bondage as slaves in the land of Egypt. When God finally decided to deliver the children of Israel out of slavery, God spoke to all the people of Israel with his own voice so that they would know that the God who delivered them out of Egypt was a living God.

Before God allowed all the people of Israel to hear his voice, God used Moses to be his personal spokesman to them (Exo. 4:10-16). Although Moses was their leader when they escaped from Egypt, the people of Israel, in their stubbornness, began to question Moses' authority. Therefore, God told Moses to gather the whole congregation before Mount Sinai in Horeb, and he would speak to them himself.

After three days, God appeared on Mount Sinai in a great storm of fire. God did not allow anyone to remain on the mountain, not even Moses, his most trusted servant. God spoke to all the children of Israel, saying, "**I *am* the LORD thy God, which have brought thee out of the land of Egypt, out of the house of bondage. #1) Thou shalt have no other gods before me. #2) Thou shalt not make unto thee any graven image, or any likeness *of any thing* that *is* in heaven above, or that *is* in the earth beneath, or that *is* in the water under the earth: Thou shalt not bow down thyself to them, nor serve them: for I the LORD thy God *am* a jealous God, visiting the iniquity of the fathers upon the children unto the third and fourth *generation* of them that hate me; And shewing mercy unto thousands of them that love me, and keep my commandments. #3) Thou shalt not take the name of the LORD thy God in vain; for the LORD will not hold him guiltless that taketh his name in vain. #4) Remember the sabbath day, to keep it holy. Six days shalt thou labour, and do all thy work: But the seventh day *is* the sabbath of the LORD thy God: *in it* thou shalt not do any work, thou, nor thy son, nor thy daughter, thy manservant, nor thy maidservant, nor thy cattle, nor thy stranger that *is* within thy gates: For *in* six days(ages) the LORD made heaven and earth, the sea, and all that in them *is,* and rested the seventh day(age): wherefore the LORD blessed the sabbath day, and hallowed it. #5) Honour thy father and thy mother: that thy days may be long upon the land which the LORD thy God giveth thee. #6) Thou shalt not kill. #7) Thou shalt not commit adultery. #8) Thou shalt not steal. #9) Thou shalt not bear false witness against thy neighbour. #10) Thou shalt not covet thy neighbour's house, thou shalt not covet thy neighbour's wife, nor his manservant, nor his maidservant, nor his ox, nor his ass, or any thing that *is* thy

neighbour's [Exo. 20:2-17]." The two great commandments that Jesus Christ spoke of were not mentioned among the Ten Commandments that God declared to the children of Israel with his own voice.

* * *

Jesus Christ said that the commandment of "Thou shalt love thy neighbour as thyself" is the second of the two great commandments. But the words "Thou shalt love thy neighbour as thyself" was spoken forty years before Moses declared that the children of Israel should love God with all their heart and mind: which would ultimately be declared the greatest of all the commandments.

The book of Leviticus was so named after the tribe of Levi. The Levites were the tribe that God ordained to be the priests and ministers to the children of Israel (Num. 3:1-7). It is within the book of Leviticus where the second greatest commandment was spoken by Moses.

We are very familiar with the words, "Thou shalt love thy neighbour as thyself," but what most do not know is that there are many other commandments that introduce these words. These commandments helped to establish an image of what it truly is to love thy neighbor as thyself. The commandments that introduce this concept describes how the children of Israel were to love one another collectively as if they were showing love to themselves individually. The only neighbor the children of Israel would respect were their flesh and blood family member and those who lived among them who had accepted the law of Moses (Exo. 12:48 / Deu. 7:1-6). The other nations and races were not considered neighbors in the eyes of the Israelite people.

Moses explained to the people of Israel that God required them to be holy before him. Therefore, Moses began to teach the people what would be accepted as an example of loving your neighbor in this manner, saying, "**And when ye reap the harvest of your land, thou shalt not wholly**(completely) **reap the corners of thy field, neither shalt thou gather the gleanings**(small portions) **of thy harvest. And thou shalt not glean**(gather bit by bit) **thy vineyard, neither shalt thou gather *every* grape of thy vineyard; thou shalt leave them for the poor and** stranger: I *am* the LORD your God. Ye shall not steal, neither deal falsely, neither lie one to another. And ye shall not swear by my name falsely, neither shalt thou profane the name of thy God: I *am* the LORD. Thou shalt not defraud thy neighbour, neither rob *him:* the wages of him that is hired shall not abide with thee all night until the morning. Thou shalt not curse(despise) the deaf, nor put a stumbling block before the blind, but shalt fear thy God: I *am* the LORD. Ye shall do no unrighteousness in judgment: thou shalt not respect the person of the poor, nor honour the person of the mighty: *but* in righteousness shalt thou judge thy neighbour. Thou shalt not go up and down *as* a talebearer(slanderer) among thy people: neither shalt thou stand against the blood(innocent) of thy neighbour; I *am* the LORD. Thou shalt not hate thy brother in thine heart: thou shalt in any wise rebuke thy neighbour, and not suffer(allow) sin upon him. Thou shalt not avenge, nor bear any grudge against the children of thy people, but thou shalt love thy neighbour as thyself: I *am* the LORD [Lev. 19:9-18]." The children of Israel now had a standard in place that gave them an image of the love they were to share among one another.

* * *

It was not long after Moses taught the children of Israel how to love one another that they rebelled against God and were forced to wander in the wilderness for thirty-eight more years (Num. 13-14). For thirty-eight years, God allowed the people to worship all sorts of pagan gods (Amos 5:25-26 / Acts 7:41-43); and none of their newborn children were taught the customs of the law that Moses had given to them (Jos. 5:2-7).

After forty years of wandering in the wilderness, God finally allowed the people of Israel to go over into the land that he promised to give to them. While the people prepared to cross over the Jordan River and enter the land of Canaan, Moses once again declared to the people all the commandments of God.

Moses began by reminding the children of Israel of all the things they had been through for the last forty years. Then he said, "**NOW these *are* the commandments, the statutes, and the judgments, which the LORD your God commanded to teach you, that ye might do *them* in the land whither**(where) **ye go to possess it: That thou mightest fear the LORD thy God, to keep all his statutes and his commandments, which I command thee, thou, and thy son, and thy son's son, all the days of thy life; and that thy days may be prolonged. Hear therefore, O Israel, and observe to do *it;* that it may be well with thee, and that ye may increase mightily, as the LORD God of thy fathers hath promised thee, in the land that floweth with milk and honey. Hear, O Israel: The LORD our God *is* one LORD: And thou shalt love the LORD thy God with all thine heart, and with all thy soul, and with all thy might. And these words, which I command thee this day, shall be in thine heart: And thou shalt teach them diligently unto thy children, and shalt talk of them when thou sittest in thine house, and when thou walkest by the way, and when thou liest down, and when thou risest up** [Deu. 6:1-7]." After many years of worshiping everything else besides the living God, Moses was reminding the people that there is only one God and that loving the one and only living God with all their heart would prolong their days in the land of Canaan.

* * *

The two greatest commandments were spoken forty years apart from one another. Before the children of Israel wandered in the wilderness for forty years, Moses declared to them how they were to love one another. After forty years of wandering around in circles, Moses declared that they were to love the LORD thy God with all their heart, and with all their soul, and with all their strength above anyone or anything. These two commandments were not a part of the original Ten Commandments that God spoke to all the people with his own voice on Mount Horeb because these two commandments far exceed the daily sacrifices that are contained within the law of Moses.

Jesus Christ acknowledged these two commandments and understood the significance of declaring them both as the greatest commandments of all. The two greatest commandments bring with them the responsibility of acknowledging God in all our ways and doing to others as we would have others do unto us. These two commandments help us to receive a new level of respect for all of God's creation. The religious organizations of Christ's generation ignored these two commandments and accepted the portion of the Old Testament law that benefited their own selfish agendas.

Our goal within the New Testament should be to open our hearts and strive to become one with the greatest commandments. In order to become one with the two greatest commandments of all, we must first learn the value of overcoming the moral challenges that face us based on the original Ten Commandments. Then we will be able to move forward and understand how to become living sacrifices as was Jesus Christ. The Ten Commandments are holy and just, but the two greatest commandments are righteous. Fulfilling these two great commandments by following the example of Jesus Christ will allow our behavior to confess to all the world that the spirit of Jesus Christ dwells within our hearts. The two greatest commandments have just been revealed in Divine Context.

Context #6 reveals how God allowed Moses to understand the things that pertain to the Old Testament, but not the things that pertain to the New Testament.

EXODUS 33:20-23

20. And he(God) said, Thou(Moses) canst not see my face: for there shall no man see me, and live.
21. And the LORD said, Behold, *there is* a place by me, and thou shalt stand upon a rock:
22. And it shall come to pass, while my glory passeth by, that I will put thee in a clift of the rock, and will cover thee with my hand while I pass by:
23. And I will take away mine hand, and thou shalt see my back parts: but my face shall not be seen.

The Back Parts Of God

Divine Context is understanding that God was not speaking to Moses about his face and his back parts in a fleshly manner. God was saying to Moses that he would reveal to him the glory of his covenant concerning the children of Israel, which is now considered to be the Old Testament, but he would not reveal to Moses the glory of his covenant concerning all of mankind, which is the New Testament.

* * *

Hearing God speak words referring to his face and his back can send our thoughts reeling, trying to grasp exactly what these words really mean. God's face must be awesome, and God's back parts cannot be too far behind in magnificence. God's back parts were all that Moses got the chance to see. Seeing God's back parts were sufficient for Moses to be convinced that God would do all that he said concerning the children of Israel.

Moses was born into the Hebrew family of the Levites, while the children of Israel were slaves in the land of Egypt. Moses survived by the grace of God because, at his birth, death was supposed to follow close behind. Pharaoh had commanded his Egyptian servants to kill all the male children born to the Hebrew women. Due to this decree, Moses' parents hid him for three months. They then made a small vessel and put Moses in the river, hoping that somehow good fortune would find him. Good fortune came in the form of Pharoah's own daughter, who found Moses in the river and decided to raise him as her own son (Exo. 2:1-10).

For many generations, the Egyptians held dominion over the Israelites. Through their forefather Jacob(Israel) and through Jacob's son Joseph, the people of Israel came to Egypt on joyous terms. After a few hundred years, the people of Israel had been turned into slaves, ruled by an oppressive king of Egypt. The Israelites multiplied so rapidly that the king of Egypt began to kill the male children as soon as they were born. It was time for God to intervene and start the process of deliverance. This process began with the birth of Moses.

When Moses was forty years old, he decided to do something about Pharaoh's oppression of his kindred. One day when Moses saw an Egyptian abusing an Israelite, Moses became angry and killed the Egyptian. The next day, Moses heard that Pharaoh knew that he had murdered one of his servants, and in his fear, Moses fled to the land of Midian.

After remaining in the land of Midian for forty years, Moses, at the age of eighty, was tending to his father-in-law's flock near mount Horeb when the angel(word) of God appeared to him in a burning bush and said, "**I have surely seen the affliction of my people which *are* in Egypt, and have heard their cry by reason of their taskmasters; for I know their sorrows; And I am come down to deliver them out of the hand of the Egyptians, and to bring them up out of that land unto a good land and a large, unto a land flowing with milk and honey; unto the place of the Canaanites, and the Hittites, and the Amorites, and the Perizzites, and the Hivites, and the Jebusites. Now therefore, behold, the cry of the children of Israel is come unto me: and I have also seen the oppression wherewith the Egyptians oppress them. Come now therefore, and I will send thee unto Pharaoh, that thou mayest bring forth my people the children of Israel out of Egypt [Exo. 3:7-10].**"

This idea did not sound good to Moses. Therefore, Moses began to make all kinds of excuses for why he would not be a good candidate to bring the people of Israel out of Egypt. After wrestling with Moses for a while, God finally told Moses that his older brother Aaron would assist him in the mission. After seeing his brother Aaron, they both went to the elders of the Israelites and told them all the things that the LORD had said about delivering the children of Israel from out of the land of Egypt. The Israelites were glad to hear this, and they bowed their heads and thanked God. But things would become much worse for the people of Israel before they became better.

Pharaoh began to oppress the children of Israel even more once he heard that they desired to go out into the wilderness to meet their God. Because of this, it became an uphill battle as Moses tried to convince the Israelites that God had finally decided to show them favor. The mission seemed impossible. The people of Israel were not warriors. They were abused slaves and servants who had yielded to the authority of Pharaoh and the Egyptians all their lives. If being delivered out of Egypt was left up to the Israelites, they would perhaps still have been servants to the Egyptians for many more years. Nevertheless, it was not left up to them. This was God's plan, and God's doing.

It came to pass that God used Aaron and Moses to destroy the land of Egypt with many different signs and wonders. It was not that God was trying to persuade the Egyptians to let his people go, as much as God was trying to convince his own people that he was God. God turned rivers into blood, filled the homes of the Egyptians with frogs, put lice in their hair, sent swarms of flies to torment them, allowed infectious diseases to ravage them and their livestock, rained down hail and lightning from the sky that ruined their crops, sent locust among them to consume all that was left of their vegetation, and brought a darkness over their land that could be felt (Exo. 7-11).

All these signs were carried out on the Egyptians by Moses through the power of God, but there was one last plague: a plague that would cripple the Egyptians for a whole generation. God brought evil angels into Egypt and killed all the firstborn males of every Egyptian, man and beast (Exo. 12:29). The horrors of death even found their way into the house of Pharaoh. Pharaoh then called for Moses and told him to gather his people and all their possessions and leave immediately.

The Egyptians were distraught, to say the least, and allowed anyone else who wanted to leave with the Israelites to exit. There was a mixed multitude of different nationalities that jumped at the chance to depart from under the iron fist of Pharaoh (Exo. 12:38). As the people began to leave, Pharaoh reconsidered. Pharaoh changed his mind and chased after all the people. God assisted Pharaoh's efforts by hardening Pharaoh's heart so that he could not stand the sight of all those slaves getting away. As Pharaoh chased after the people, God opened the Red Sea and allowed the children of Israel, along with the others, to cross over the sea on dry ground. Pharaoh, in his madness, gathered his greatest soldiers and followed the Israelites into the sea. The waters came together again, and Pharaoh and all his men drowned in the Red Sea. When the children of Israel saw this, they danced and sang a song to the LORD.

* * *

The children of Israel were free, but they were still blind to what freedom really was. They were also still ignorant of who God really was, although it was God that had delivered them out of bondage. Regardless of what Moses said to the people, God knew that there was only one way for them to understand and believe that he was the one and only living God. Therefore, after the people murmured against Moses and Aaron a few times about bringing them into the wilderness, God decided to do something that had never been done before. God pushed Moses away and made Moses go down to the bottom of the mountain and stand with all the people while he spoke to everyone with his own voice from the mountaintop.

Moses was told by God to gather everyone together, and in three days, he would speak to them. On the third day, God spoke to all the people as one. God spoke the Ten Commandments to all who were present. When they heard God's voice, all the people became afraid and said to Moses, "**Speak thou with us, and we will hear: but let not God speak with us, lest we die** [Exo. 20:19]." Moses tried to calm them down by saying, "**Fear not: for God is come to prove you, and that his fear may be before your faces, that ye sin not** [Exo. 20:20]." The people were not buying it. They backed away from the mountain and stood afar off.

Moses then went up on the mountain where the presence of God was. From this point forward, God only spoke to Moses. Moses would be God's voice to the people. While on the mountain, God gave Moses many judgments that would bring civility and fairness to the everyday lives of these twelve tribes and to the mixed multitude that had chosen to join them (Exo. 21-23).

Once Moses returned to the camp, he told everyone about the judgments that God had given him concerning them all. The people of Israel responded to Moses, saying, "**All the words which the LORD hath said will we do** [Exo. 24:3]." Moses wrote all the words that God had spoken to him in a book. Moses then repeated these words to the audience that gathered with him the next morning. Moses also sprinkled the book and the people with the blood of the sacrifices that had been offered to God and said to them, "**Behold the blood of the covenant, which the LORD hath made with you concerning all these words** [Exo. 24:8]."

When Moses was finished speaking to the people about all the commandments that God had given him, Moses again went up on the mountain where the presence of God was. Moses remained there for forty days and forty nights. During these forty days and forty nights, God spoke to Moses about how to construct the tabernacle and the manner of the services that accompanied it. The only other thing that God mentioned to Moses was the responsibilities of the sabbath day. God wanted the tabernacle to be perfect according to all that he said to Moses (Exo. 25-31).

While Moses was on the mountain with God, things became chaotic back in the camp where the rest of the Israelites were. They put the press on Aaron, saying to him, "**Up, make us gods, which shall go before us; for *as for* this Moses, the man that brought us up out of the land of Egypt, we wot**(know) **not what is become of him** [Exo. 32:1]." Aaron feared the people and gave in to their desires. Cattle were considered sacred in the land of Egypt, where the Israelites had just escaped from (Gen. 46:33-34 / Exo. 8:25-26). So, Aaron took their jewelry and made a golden calf. Once the elders of Israel saw the golden calf, they all said to the rest of the people, "**These *be* thy gods, O Israel, which brought thee up out of the land of Egypt** [Exo. 32:4]."

Forty days was just too much. The people could not take it anymore. They were all stuck out in the wilderness eating manna for bread and quails for meat (Exo. 16:11-15). Although they had seen the destruction that God brought on the Egyptians, the curse of Adam became dominant and caused them to rebel against the word of God. They had also heard the voice of God speaking from the mountaintop that burned with fire and begged Moses to speak to God on their behalf because the voice of God was too much for them to bear. Even with all these experiences, they still rebelled against the commandments that God had spoken to them.

The family of the Israelites were slaves, recently rescued from under the powerful hand of the king of Egypt. All the people who were present knew only oppression. Moses was put in charge of a collective group of individuals that had been abused their entire lives. Hope was nothing for them to be fond of, and believing in someone or something would only last for a while. So, when Moses went up into the mountain, it took him too long to return. The people became restless and decided that they would take over. They were all ignorant of the consequences of their actions.

Moses was God's man. Moses was the one who God had come to and convinced that he was able to lead his people out from the land of Egypt. For Moses, God's presence was welcoming. Moses and God had built a relationship that afforded Moses to trust that God was a living God. Moses understood the consequences of rebelling against God. He also understood the benefits of believing in and obeying God.

Blind to all that was taking place back in the camp, Moses humbly remained on the mountain with God for forty days and forty nights. God is all-knowing, and when God saw the foolishness of the people, he said to Moses, "**Go, get thee down; for thy people, which thou broughtest out of the land of Egypt, have corrupted *themselves:* They** have turned aside quickly out of the way which I commanded them: they have made them a molten calf, and have worshiped it, and have sacrificed thereunto, and said, These *be* thy gods, O Israel, which have brought thee up out of the land of Egypt. And the LORD said unto Moses, I have seen this people, and, behold, it *is* a stiffnecked people: Now therefore let me alone, that my wrath may wax hot against them, and that I may consume them: and I will make of thee a great nation** [Exo. 32:7-10]."

God was angry and wanted to destroy all the people back in the camp. They had broken the covenant between themselves and God in less than two months. God was ready to pour out his anger on all the people and demolish them in an instant. However, God could not do it while Moses was in his presence. Moses had power with God. If none of the other people believed in God, God knew that Moses did. Moses could have been selfish and taken the offer of God to make "of him" a great nation, but Moses was faithful on both ends. Moses was faithful to God as a servant, and Moses was also faithful to the children of Israel as their leader. Moses did not want God to destroy them. There was no doubt about the intimate relationship that Moses and God had built throughout this whole deliverance process. Moses had also built an intimate relationship with all his kindred, so he could not let God go out like that. Moses used his influence to persuade God not to destroy his own people.

When God asked Moses to leave from off the mountain and get out of his presence so that he could destroy the people, Moses did not budge. Moses stood before God and begged God not to forget his own words, saying, "**LORD, why doth thy wrath wax hot against thy people, which thou hast brought forth out of the land of Egypt with great power, and with a mighty hand? Wherefore should the Egyptians speak, and say, For mischief did he**(God) **bring them out, to slay them in the mountains, and to consume them from the face of the earth? Turn from thy fierce wrath, and repent of this evil against thy people. Remember Abraham, Isaac, and Israel, thy servants, to whom thou swarest by thine own self, and saidst, unto them, I will multiply your seed as the stars of heaven, and all this land that I have**

spoken of will I give unto your seed, and they shall inherit *it* forever [Exo. 32:11-13]."

God listened to all that Moses said. It was God's own words that Moses used to convince God not to destroy all the people. It was an amazing thing to see God change his course because of the cries of a mortal man. This gave Moses confidence that he could communicate with God, and in return, God would consider all that he had to say.

* * *

After Moses calmed the wrath of God, he left the mountain and returned to the camp. Moses found the people celebrating their hand-crafted god. The LORD had written ten commandments on two stone tablets and given them to Moses while he was up on the mountain. These ten commandments were written in stone by God so that the people could always remember the voice of God. When Moses came to the bottom of the mountain and saw that the people had indeed made a golden calf to worship as their god, Moses threw the two stone tablets to the ground and broke them (Exo. 32:19).

There was no use in trying to talk to the people anymore. Something drastic had to be done. Moses made them destroy the golden calf. Then the tribe of Levi joined Moses' cause and killed about three thousand men who participated in the idolatry (Exo. 32:26-28). It was a sad day for Moses and the people. They lost some of their family members, but the small portion that died that day was nothing compared to what God wanted to do to them all. Moses was not ignorant of the displeasure of God towards all the people, and Moses also knew that he would have to face God once again on their behalf. Therefore, Moses said to them, **"Ye have sinned a great sin: and now I will go up unto the LORD; peradventure**(perhaps) **I shall make an atonement for your sin** [Exo. 32:30]."

Moses went up on the mountain again and entered the presence of God. As Moses began to plead for God to have mercy on his kindred, Moses put his own life on the line to save them from God's wrath. Knowing that God yielded to his cries once before, Moses tried his hand again with the LORD, saying, "**Oh, this people have sinned a great sin, and have made them gods of gold. Yet now, if thou wilt forgive their sin-; and if not, blot me, I pray thee, out of thy book which thou hast written** [Exo. 32:31-32]."

God was not going to hear all that Moses asked of him this time. It was not about Moses; it was about God. God responded to Moses' request to blot him out of his book, saying, "**Whosoever hath sinned against me, him will I blot out of my book. Therefore now go, lead the people unto *the place* of which I have spoken unto thee: behold, mine Angel shall go before thee: nevertheless in the day when I visit I will visit their sin upon them** [Exo. 32:33-34]." "**Depart, *and* go up hence, thou and the people which thou hast brought up out of the land of Egypt, unto the land which I sware unto Abraham, to Isaac, and to Jacob, saying, Unto thy seed will I give it: And I will send an angel**(messenger) **before thee; and I will drive out the Canaanite, the Amorite, and the Hittite, and the Perizzite, and the Hivite, and the Jebusite: Unto a land flowing with milk and honey: for I will not go up in the mist of thee; for thou *art* a stiffnecked people: lest I consume thee in the way** [Exo. 33:1-3]." When Moses returned to the camp, he told the people that God was not going with them into the promised land because they had rejected God by worshiping the golden calf. Moses took up the tabernacle from among them and placed it far off from the congregation. Moses and God then communed concerning the people's fate. For the scripture says, "**And the LORD spake unto Moses face**(will) **to face**(will)**, as a man speaketh unto his friend** [Exo. 33:11]." At this point, God was willing to reveal his feelings to Moses concerning the condition of the people, and Moses was there to remind God that they were his people, the people that he chose.

God told Moses that he would not go up with the people into the land of Canaan. Moses knew that he could not do this all alone. Moses understood that he was simply a servant. His leadership came about only through the relationship that he and God had developed. Without God, nothing would go as planned; only God could back him up as he wrestled with the people night and day. With God speaking to Moses will to will as his friend, Moses felt compelled to ask God not to send him on an impossible mission, saying, "**See, thou sayest unto me, Bring up this people: and thou hast not let me know whom thou wilt send with me. Yet thou hast said, I know thee by name, and thou hast also found grace in my sight. Now therefore, I pray thee, if I have found grace in thy sight, shew**(show) **me now thy way**(will)**, that I may know thee, that I may find grace in thy sight: and consider that this nation** *is* **thy people** [Exo. 33:12-13]." God is a God of mercy, and he could not break his friend's heart by leaving him to deal with this enormous task all alone. God felt Moses' pain. Therefore, God said to Moses, "**My presence shall go** *with thee,* **and I will give thee rest** [Exo. 33:14]."

Moses then responded to God, saying, "**If thy presence go not** *with me,* **carry us not up hence. For wherein shall it be known here that I and thy people have found grace in thy sight?** *is it* **not in that thou goest with us? so shall we be separated, I and thy people, from all the people that** *are* **upon the face of the earth** [Exo. 33:15-16]." As Moses poured out his heart to God, God gave in and said to him, "**I will do this thing also that thou hast spoken: for thou hast found grace in my sight, and I know thee by name** [Exo. 33:17]." Moses was not going to cut himself short. While Moses had the wind at his back, he was going to use all this momentum to get all that he could out of God. God and Moses had shared a moment, and Moses was not ready for this moment to end just yet. Knowing that God granted him a request once before, Moses asked for it all, saying, "**I beseech thee, shew me thy glory** [Exo. 33:18]."

It was too late for God to turn back. Moses, in his humble sincerity, had found God's soft spot. God yielded to Moses' request and began to prepare Moses for everything that he would learn of his will for the next forty days and nights. God said to Moses, "**I will make all my goodness pass before thee, and I will proclaim the name of the LORD before thee; and will be gracious to whom I will be gracious, and I will shew mercy on whom I will shew mercy. . . . Thou canst not see**(discern) **my face**(complete will)**: for there shall no man see me**(my complete will)**, and live. . . . Behold,** *there is* **a place by me, and thou shalt stand upon a rock**(mountain)**: And it shall come to pass, while my**

glory passeth by, that I will put thee in a clift of the rock, and will cover thee with my hand(power) **while I pass by: And I will take away mine hand**(power)**, and thou shalt see my back parts: but my face shall not be seen** [Exo. 33:19-23]."

The LORD told Moses to cut out two stone tablets like the first two that he broke when he saw the people worshiping the golden calf (Exo. 34:1). The conversation that God and Moses were having concerning God's glory took place inside the tabernacle at the bottom of the mountain. For Moses to see a portion of God's glory, he would have to go up on the mountain once again.

When Moses entered into God's presence the next morning on the mountain, "**. . . the LORD descended in the cloud, and stood**(presented himself) **with him there, and proclaimed the name of the LORD. And the LORD passed by before him**(Moses)**, and proclaimed, The LORD, The LORD God, merciful and gracious, longsuffering, and abundant in goodness and truth, Keeping mercy for thousands, forgiving iniquity and transgression and sin, and that will by no means clear** *the guilty;* **visiting the iniquity of the fathers upon the children, and upon the children's children, unto the third and to the fourth** *generation.* **And Moses made haste, and bowed his head toward the earth, and worshipped. And he**(Moses) **said, If now I have found grace in thy sight, O Lord, let my Lord, I pray thee, go among us; for it** *is* **a stiffnecked**(stubborn) **people; and pardon our iniquity and our sin, and take us for thine inheritance. And he**(God) **said, Behold, I make a covenant: before all thy people I will do marvels, such as have not been done in all the earth, nor in any nation: and all the people among which thou** *art* **shall see the work of the LORD: for it** *is* **a terrible**(fearful) **thing that I will do with thee. Observe thou that which I command thee this day: behold, I drive out before thee the Amorite, and the Canaanite, and the Hittite, and the Perizzite, and the Hivite, and the Jebusite. Take heed to thyself, lest thou make a covenant with the inhabitants of the land whither**(where) **thou goest, lest it be for a snare in the midst of thee: But ye shall destroy their altars, break their images, and cut down their groves: For thou shalt worship no other god: for the LORD,** whose name *is* Jealous, *is* a jealous God: Lest thou make a covenant with the inhabitants of the land, and they go a whoring after their gods, and do sacrifice unto their gods, and *one* call thee, and thou eat of his sacrifice; And thou take of their daughters unto thy sons, and their daughters go a whoring after their gods, and make thy sons go a whoring after their gods. Thou shalt make thee no molten gods. The feast of unleavened bread shalt thou keep. Seven days thou shalt eat unleavened bread, as I commanded thee, in the time of the month Abib: for in the month Abib thou camest out from Egypt. All that openeth the matrix *is* mine; and every firstling among thy cattle, *whether* ox or sheep, *that is male*. But the firstling of an ass thou shalt redeem with a lamb: and if thou redeem *him* not, then shalt thou break his neck. All the firstborn of thy sons thou shalt redeem. And none shall appear before me empty. Six days thou shalt work, but on the seventh day thou shalt rest: in earing time and in harvest thou shalt rest. And thou shalt observe the feast of weeks, of the firstfruits of the wheat harvest, and the feast of ingathering at the year's end. Thrice(three times) in the year shall all your men children appear before the Lord GOD, the God of Israel. For I will cast out the nations before thee, and enlarge thy borders: neither shall any man desire thy land, when thou shalt go up to appear before the LORD thy God thrice in the year. Thou shalt not offer the blood of my sacrifice with leaven; neither shall the sacrifice of the feast of the passover be left unto the mourning. The first of the firstfruits of thy land thou shalt bring unto the house of the LORD thy God. Thou shalt not seethe(boil) a kid(young livestock) in his mother's milk. . . . Write thou these words: for after the tenor(portion) of these words I have made a covenant with thee and with Israel [Exo. 34:5-27]."

The covenant that God had just spoken to Moses represents God's back parts. There were many other things that God would add to this covenant over the years, but for the most part, these few words that were spoken to Moses at this moment established the foundation for the Old Testament law. For the second time, Moses stayed on the mountain with God for forty days and forty nights. Moses did not eat or drink anything. God filled Moses with all his will concerning the children of Israel: all that he would do for them, all that he would do to them, and all that he would do with them. Once again, God also wrote on the two stone tablets those original ten commandments that he spoke to the people with his own voice.

When Moses came down from the mountain, the skin of his face shined so bright that as he spoke with the people, they were afraid to come near him (Exo. 34:29-35). Moses had to put a veil over his face as he relayed to them the commandments of the LORD. The only time that Moses removed the veil was when he went into the tabernacle to speak with God. At no other time did Moses' face shine after returning from the presence of God. This time things were different. This time, God revealed to Moses his plans for the children of Israel and sealed those plans within Moses' heart and mind.

* * *

God showed Moses his back parts but not his face. God's back parts represent the Old Testament. The Old Testament (the law of Moses, to be exact) contains the will of God concerning the children of Israel. There are specks of prophecy pertaining to Jesus Christ and the New Testament era sprinkled throughout the first five books of the Bible (Gen. 3:14-15/17:4-5 / Deu. 18:15-19), but the law of Moses is dominated by the history of what God did for the Israelites and what God expected from the Israelites in return.

The back parts of God that Moses was allowed to understand(see) was God's immediate will for the children of Israel. The Old Testament is referred to as God's back parts because, in the overall scheme of God's will, the laws and the customs that were designed to justify the flesh(Israelites) would, in due time, become inferior to the righteousness of Jesus Christ. The law of Moses would eventually become the portion of God's will that is less significant than the more glorious portion of God's will that was to come.

The revealing of God's face, that is, the revealing of the New Testament, made it clear that the Old Testament (God's back) was only put in place as a foundation that would help to legitimize and support the New Testament. The old law would become the lesser of the two. It would become the rear, the former standard that was founded to last but for a moment in time.

God did not reveal his face to Moses. God did not reveal to Moses the most significant portion of his will that was reserved for another generation and era (Acts 3:22-26). There was no need to fill Moses with all this information. The time of Jesus Christ was far off, and the things that were taking place at that time were all that needed to be established in order to help Moses understand the will of God for the Israelites.

God allowed Moses to feel his power and understand what mattered the most at that moment. This is the reason why God said to Moses beforehand, "**And it shall come to pass, while my glory**(Spirit) **passeth by, that I will put thee in a clift of the rock**(mountain), **and will cover**(join) **thee with my hand**(power) **while I pass by: And I will take away mine hand**(power), **and thou shalt see**(discern) **my back parts**(present covenant): **but my face**(future covenant) **shall not be seen** [Exo. 33:22-23]."

When God spoke to Moses, saying, "**Thou canst not see my face: for there shall no man see me, and live** [Exo. 33:20]," God was not speaking about his face as in a fleshly manner. God's power, God's splendor, and God's greatness are revealed by God's prediction of the New Testament and by God's fulfillment of the New Testament. God's face represents God's complete will, God's perfect will, and God's eternal will, which is the same will that included the cancellation of the covenant that God made with Moses in order to solidify the testimony of Jesus Christ (Heb. 7:18-19). The revelation of the New Testament would have been too much for Moses to handle. Moses was already struggling with the things that pertained to that present time. The future covenant, which is God's face, would be revealed when God was ready to do so.

Moreover, God was not referring to someone literally falling dead upon seeing his face. The New Testament reveals that all those who received the gift of the Holy Ghost turned away from their selfish desires and began to follow the example of Jesus Christ (Rom. 6:3-7). For a person to see God's face and not be able to live is a saying that is difficult to grasp without spiritual discernment. Jesus Christ understood exactly what this meant. When Jesus told his disciples that the Jews were going to crucify him, Peter began to rebuke Christ for even suggesting such a thing could take place (Mat. 16:22). Peter did not want to hear this kind of talk and wanted Christ to know how he felt. As he responded to Peter, the words of Jesus Christ give us a detailed image of what must first take place within our hearts for us to understand the eternal will of God. Christ responded to Peter's thoughts aggressively, saying, **"Get thee behind me, Satan: thou art an offence unto me: for thou savourest**(desire) **not the things that be of God**(God's will)**, but those that be of men**(man's will)**. Then said Jesus unto his disciples, If any *man* will come after me, let him deny himself, and take up his cross**(calling)**, and follow me. For whosoever will save his life shall lose it: and whosoever will lose his life for my sake shall find it** [Mat. 16:23-25]." If Peter wanted to recognize God's eternal will, he would have to deny his own desires and obey all that Jesus Christ had taught him concerning God's will.

* * *

Moses wanted God to show him his glory. God granted Moses his wish. But God only allowed his power to reveal to Moses the things that pertain to his covenant with the children of Israel: to give to them the land that he promised to their forefathers. When we hear of the face of God, we must not allow our thoughts to become mangled, distorting the true context and the very image of what is truly being said at that time. There are a few instances within the Bible where individuals confessed to seeing God, and their lives were spared. Jacob said to Esau, his brother, that seeing his face was like seeing the face of God because God had revealed to Jacob beforehand that he would resolve the conflict between him and his brother Esau. When God revealed himself to Jacob during prayer, Jacob called the name of the place Peniel, saying, "**. . . for I have seen God face to face, and my life is preserved** [Gen. 32:30]." And again, when the angel of God spoke to the parents of Samson, afterward Samson's father, Manoah, said to his wife, "**We shall surely die,** because we have seen God. But his wife said unto him, If the LORD were pleased to kill us, he would not have received a burnt offering and a meat offering at our hands, neither would he have shewed us all these *things,* nor would as at this time have told us *such things* as these** [Judg. 13:22-23]." Here we can recognize that neither Jacob nor Samson's father, Manoah saw God's face literally. What they did get the chance to understand was God's will concerning their situations.

Although Moses only got the chance to see God's back, it was so pure that Moses had to put a veil over his face. The people were afraid to look at Moses. The covenant that God made with the children of Israel was glorious. It was so glorious, in fact, that the covenant of God even frightened those who were the direct beneficiaries of it.

The ushering in of the New Testament snatched the veil off Moses' face and exposed the weakness of the law(glory) that once held dominion over the people of Israel. The Apostle Paul wrote of this very same thing in his second letter to the Corinthians. In Paul's comparison of the glory of the New Testament as opposed to the glory of the Old Testament, he explained that justification according to the Old Testament law was done away with in Jesus Christ.

Paul gives an example of how the New Testament messengers do not have to hide behind a veil as Moses did. The will of God, according to the testimony of Jesus Christ, is easy to accept if we have an open heart. The covenant that God made with Moses was glorious, but now that the face of God has shown itself through a new and improved covenant, God's back parts are less glorious when compared to the glory of the covenant that came after. Paul explains this to the Corinthians, saying, "**For even that**(God's back parts) **which was made glorious had no glory in this respect, by reason of the glory**(God's face) **that excelleth. For if that**(the Old Testament) **which is done away *was* glorious, much more that**(the New Testament) **which remaineth *is* glorious. Seeing then that we**(the apostles) **have such hope, we**(the apostles) **use great plainness of speech: And not as Moses, *which* put a vail over his face, that the children of Israel could not steadfastly**(sincerely) **look to the end of that**(God's back parts) **which is abolished: But their minds were blinded: for until this day remaineth the same vail untaken**

away in the reading of the old testament; which *vail* is done away in Christ. But even unto this day, when Moses(the Old Testament) **is read, the vail is upon their heart. Nevertheless, when it**(their heart) **shall turn to the Lord, the vail shall be taken away** [2 Cor. 3:10-16]."

The back parts of God that Moses was allowed to see(understand) is simply a metaphor used in reference to the Old Testament law, which consisted of the covenant that God made with the children of Israel through Moses. God's face, on the other hand, is the New Testament principles that are placed within our hearts and within our minds, inspiring us to deny our own personal self-righteousness and follow the example of Jesus Christ.

Moses went through a lot in the wilderness. Moses had to learn how to put up with all the complaining of the people of Israel and remain sincere in the sight of God. God was gracious to Moses and filled Moses with the glory of his will for the people of Israel. God reserved a portion of that glory: the glory that would allow all the New Testament believers to experience God's grace from within. God is wise in his ways and blameless in his reasons. At that time, Moses received the chance to see God's back(old law), and now the Holy Ghost-filled saints have received the chance to see God's face(new law) because of the faithfulness of Moses. Thanks be to God for his infinite wisdom, his undeniable mercy, and his perfect will. The back parts of God have just been revealed in Divine Context.

Context #7 reveals how Moses spoke unadvisedly with his lips, and for this reason, he and his brother Aaron was denied the opportunity to enter the promised land of milk and honey.

NUMBERS 20:7-12

7. And the LORD spake unto Moses, saying,

8. Take the rod, and gather thou the assembly together, thou, and Aaron thy brother, and speak ye unto the rock before their eyes; and it shall give forth his water, and thou shalt bring forth to them water out of the rock: so thou shalt give the congregation and their beasts drink.

9. And Moses took the rod from before the LORD, as he commanded him.

10. And Moses and Aaron gathered the congregation together before the rock, and he said unto them, Hear now, ye rebels; must we fetch you water out of this rock?

11. And Moses lifted up his hand, and with his rod he smote the rock twice: and the water came out abundantly, and the congregation drank, and their beasts *also*.

12. And the LORD spake unto Moses and Aaron, Because ye believed me not, to sanctify me in the eyes of the children of Israel, therefore ye shall not bring this congregation into the land which I have given to them.

Moses Speaks Unadvisedly With His Lips

Divine Context is understanding that Moses was not allowed to go over into the land of promise because he spoke unadvisedly with his lips, not because he hit the rock(mountain) twice after being told by God to speak to the rock.

* * *

This situation that went ill with Moses and Aaron takes place in the book of Numbers, which is so named because of the numbering of the armies of the children of Israel and the numbering of the priesthood of the Levites. After forty years in the wilderness, the children of Israel came to a place called Kadesh. While in Kadesh, Moses and Aaron's sister Mariam died. After burying Mariam, the congregation gathered themselves together against Moses and Aaron because there was no water in Kadesh for them or their livestock to drink.

Moses and Aaron then went to the door of the tabernacle of witness and prayed to God. The glory of God then appeared to them, and God said, **"Take the rod, and gather thou the assembly together, thou, and Aaron thy brother, and speak ye unto the rock**(mountain) **before their eyes: and it shall give forth his water, and thou shalt bring forth** to them water out of the rock: so shalt thou give the congregation and their beasts drink. And Moses took the rod from before the LORD, as he commanded him** [Num. 20:8-9]."

After Moses gathered all the people together before the mountain as God told him to, Moses then said to the assembly, "**Hear now, ye rebels; must we fetch you water out of this rock? And Moses lifted up his hand, and with his rod he smote**(hit) **the rock twice: and the water came out abundantly, and the congregation drank, and their beasts** *also* [Num. 20:10-11]."

The scripture says that God told Moses to speak to the mountain in the presence of the people. However, Moses never spoke to the mountain at all. In truth, Moses spoke to the people, and then Moses lifted his hand, and with his rod, he hit the mountain twice.

Although Moses was out of order, God still allowed the mountain to give water. Immediately thereafter, God said to both Moses and Aaron, "**Because ye believed me not, to sanctify**(separate) **me in the eyes of the children of Israel, therefore ye shall not bring this congregation into the land which I have given them** [Num. 20:12]."

How did Moses and Aaron not sanctify(set apart) God before the eyes of the assembly? In looking for the answer to how Moses and Aaron did not sanctify God, we can easily say that Moses hit the mountain twice after being told by God to speak to the mountain, which was a disobedient act in the eyes of God before the children of Israel.

* * *

This situation in Kadesh was not the first time that Moses was commanded by God to retrieve water out of a mountain. Forty years earlier, the congregation being a few days removed from the land of Egypt, journeyed from the wilderness of Sin and pitched in a place called Rephidim. There was no water in Rephidim for the people to drink.

At this time also, the children of Israel argued with Moses, saying, "**Give us water that we may drink** [Exo.17:2]." Moses thought to himself, "Why are you people arguing at me, how can I give you water?" All the things that God had done in Egypt were still fresh in

Moses' mind. The children of Israel might not have considered it, but Moses surely did. Moses responded to all the people, saying, "**Why chide**(argue) **with me? wherefore do ye tempt the LORD** [Exo. 17:2]?" In the people's eyes, Moses was the teacher's pet. If the children of Israel knew nothing else, they knew this. Therefore, the people began to grumble against Moses, saying, "**Wherefore *is* this *that* thou hast brought us up out of Egypt, to kill us and our children and our cattle with thirst** [Exo. 17:3]?"

Because of the attitude of the people and their threats to stone him, Moses cried out to God. Therefore, God said to Moses, "**Go on before the people, and take with thee of the elders of Israel; and thy rod, wherewith thou smotest**(hit) **the river, take in thy hand, and go. Behold, I will stand before thee there upon the rock**(mountain) **in Horeb; and thou shalt smite**(hit) **the rock**(mountain)**, and there shall come water out of it, that the people may drink. And Moses did so in the sight of the elders of Israel** [Exo. 17:5-6]."

During this episode, to retrieve water out of the mountain in Rephidim, God told Moses to smite(hit) the mountain; God mentioned nothing about speaking to the mountain. Moses did exactly what God told him to do the first time, but forty years later, in Kadesh, Moses stepped out of order and was denied the opportunity to go over into the promised land.

The name of the place where Moses hit the mountain in Rephidim was called ". . . **Massah**(temptation)**, and Meribah**(complain)**, because of the chiding**(arguing) **of the children of Israel, and because they tempted the LORD, saying, Is the LORD among us, or not** [Exo. 17:7]?"

* * *

The difference between what took place in Rephidim not long after the children of Israel escaped out of Egypt and what took place in Kadesh forty years later is that the experience Moses had gained over that forty-year period gave him confidence to assume that he was on the same level with God in the eyes of all the people. In Kadesh, when God told Moses to speak to the mountain before the congregation, instead of speaking to the mountain in the name of the LORD, Moses, in his anger, spoke to the people, saying, "**Hear now, ye rebels; must we fetch you water out of this rock** [Num. 20:10]?"

The word "we" spoken by Moses was a show of authority on behalf of Moses and Aaron, as if they all, he, Aaron, and God, were bringing this miracle to pass. Moses did not say that it was by way of God alone that the mountain was about to give water, thereby sanctifying God in the eyes of all the assembly. This is how Moses and Aaron failed.

With Moses being the leader and Aaron being Moses' right-hand man, the words of Moses represented them both (Exo. 7:1-2). Basically, they sanctified themselves. Moses also called the congregation rebels while he and Aaron were at that very moment engaged in the manifest act of rebellion themselves.

Still, some will indeed question this interpretation and say Moses hit the mountain when he was specifically told by God to speak to the mountain, and for this reason, Moses and Aaron were not allowed to lead the congregation of Israel into the promised land. This is where the book of Psalm enters the conversation. The book of Psalm is not only a book of prophecy, but it is also a book of the testimonies of all that the children of Israel endured throughout the generations of old.

When testifying of the events that took place in the wilderness, king David says, "**They**(the children of Israel) **angered *him*(*God*) also at the waters of strife, so that it went ill with Moses for their sakes: Because they provoked his**(Moses') **spirit, so that he**(Moses) **spake**(spoke) **unadvisedly with his lips** [Psa. 106:32-33]."

The book of Psalm reveals that things went ill for Moses because "he spoke unadvisedly with his lips." While speaking to the people in Kadesh, Moses did not separate God from himself and from his brother Aaron as they went about retrieving water out of the mountain. It was God's glory that they were stealing when Moses said, " . . . must we fetch you water out of this rock?" Moses and Aaron were simply following directions: directions that they themselves asked for from God because they were frustrated with how the people were acting towards them. Saying the word "we" was an error on behalf of Moses. "We" had nothing to do with the water coming out of the mountain. It was all God's doing.

No matter if it was on purpose or not, the actions of Moses and Aaron were offensive in the sight of God. The judgment handed down to Moses and Aaron revealed that God was adamant about being sanctified apart from them, so the people of Israel would always understand that it was God who provided miracles through mankind, not mankind himself.

* * *

Through the years, Moses and Aaron endured time after time the complaints and the threats of the people of Israel (Exo. 14:12/15:24/ 16:2-3/17:2-3/32:20-21 / Num. 11:1,4-6/12:1-2/14:1-4/16:1-3/16:41). Chapter sixteen of the book of Numbers reveal that Moses and Aaron, through the help of God, had recently survived an open revolt of Korah along with two hundred and fifty princes when they attempted to take over the priesthood. God not only killed the two hundred and fifty princes along with Korah, but God also sent a plague throughout the congregation, and caused the death of over fourteen thousand people, because they blamed Moses and Aaron for the death of their family members (Num. 16:49).

Moses remained patient for forty years, but after the death of his sister Mariam, Moses was fed up when he heard the complaints of the people who said things such as, "**Would**(Wish to) **God that we had died when our brethren died before the LORD! And why have ye brought up the congregation of the LORD into this wilderness, that we and our cattle should die there? And wherefore have ye made us to come up out of Egypt, to bring us in unto this evil place? it *is* no place of seed, or of figs, or of vines, or of pomegranates; neither *is* there any water to drink** [Num. 20:3-5]." Listening to the words of the people, they felt as if it was Moses' fault that things were not going well.

Moses called the people rebels and spoke in a manner that implied that it had been he and Aaron, along with God, that provided the people with all their needs over the last forty years. Immediately, God rejected this attitude coming from the leaders of his people. To deny Moses and

Aaron the opportunity to go over into the land of promise would close all doors of complaint coming from those who thought that they could behave disobediently and still feel worthy of the promise.

The name of the place in Kadesh where Moses spoke unadvisedly was also called Meribah(complain), as in Rephidim forty years earlier because here, the children of Israel also strove with God, and he was sanctified in them. The people of Israel complained to Moses, and in doing so, they provoked Moses' spirit that he spoke unadvisedly with his lips, as Psalm 106:32-33 confirms. This is the reason why Moses and Aaron were not allowed to enter the promised land of Canaan. Moses speaks unadvisedly with his lips, has just been revealed in Divine Context.

Context #8 reveals that many of the blessings and the curses of the Old Testament should not to be applied to the New Testament generation.

DEUTERONOMY 30:19-20

19. I call heaven and earth to record this day against you, *that* I have set before you life and death, blessing and cursing: therefore choose life, that both thou and thy seed may live:

20. That thou mayest love the LORD thy God, *and* that thou mayest obey his voice, and that thou mayest cleave unto him: for he *is* thy life, and the length of thy days: that thou mayest dwell in the land which the LORD sware unto thy fathers, to Abraham, to Isaac, and to Jacob, to give them.

Blessings & Curses

Divine Context is understanding that the New Testament generation is not subject to the blessings and the curses in the book of Deuteronomy chapter 28. Those blessings and those curses came to an end when the king of Assyria destroyed the northern kingdom of Israel and when the ministry of Jesus Christ was fulfilled.

* * *

The blessings and the curses of the Old Testament book of Deuteronomy chapter 28 were given to the children of Israel in order to hold them accountable for their conduct within the land that God promised to give them. Moses spoke these words to the twelve tribes of Israel shortly before they were to cross over the Jordan river and enter the promised land of Canaan.

Moses was not allowed to cross over the Jordan River and enter the promised land because he had previously spoken unadvisedly with his lips before God (Num. 20:2-12). Because Moses knew this, God commanded him to speak to the children of Israel on a certain day concerning their responsibilities once they settled into the land.

The book of Deuteronomy is called Second Law. The commandments, the statutes, and the judgments of the book of Deuteronomy came forty years after the children of Israel were delivered out of the land of Egypt. Once God helped the children of Israel escape from Pharaoh, he gave them commandments and ordinances that they were to abide by, thus identifying them as God's peculiar people. Nevertheless, when the army was told to go and fight for the land, they became afraid of the people who occupied the land, and the army spoke evil about the land before the whole congregation. God became angry because of those men who brought up the evil report and vowed to make the children of Israel wander in the wilderness for thirty-eight more years (Num. 13-14).

Before God sealed the children of Israel's fate, they had already been in the wilderness for two years (Num. 1:1). Over the span of those two years, Moses had declared many things to them in preparation for their entrance into the promised land. God had previously spoken to them the Ten Commandments (Exo. 20:1-17), and Moses had already given them the order of the priesthood and the ordinances for all their sacrifices (Leviticus). Within those two years, the children of Israel were given laws and judgments that legitimized them as an independent nation ruled by the one and only living God. But once the mature adult males failed to believe in God and discouraged the people by refusing to go fight for the land, they were then left to themselves and forced to wander blindly in the wilderness for thirty-eight years.

During that period of thirty-eight years, none of the newborn males of the children of Israel were circumcised after the commandment of Moses (Jos. 5:5): a commandment that was a covenant given to their grandfather Abraham by God as a witness of them being his people (Gen. 17:9-14). The children that were raised up in the wilderness during this thirty-eight-year period were not taught the ways of God, but they witnessed their parents worshiping false gods such as Molech and Chiun (Amos 5:25-26). After forty years of wandering in circles, God finally ended their torment and told Moses to pass over the River Arnon. God also said to Moses at this time, "**This day will I begin to put the dread of thee and the fear of thee upon the nations** *that are* **under the whole heaven**(sky)**, who shall hear report of thee, and shall tremble, and be in anguish because of thee** [Deu. 2:25]."

After conquering the kingdoms of Og and Sihon, the children of

Israel found themselves in the plains of Moab by the Jordan River. Here Moses began to declare the second law (Deuteronomy) to them as a reminder of all that God had taken them through. Moses added even more commandments, statutes, and judgments. Along with these judgments came the declaration of the blessings and the curses that would come on the nation of Israel based on their overall conduct within the land of Canaan. All the laws, judgments, statutes, commandments, and testimonies given by Moses were to be the governing foundation of the nation of Israel. These laws and judgments could not be fully implemented until the Israelites were settled in the land as the nation of God's people.

The blessings or the curses would all come about as the result of the obedience or the disobedience of the children of Israel. The blessings and the curses were not to be accounted towards another nation or other individuals on earth that were not subject to the law of Moses. The word "if" became the deciding factor that would validate the blessings or the curses. God added the "if" factor that would ultimately decide in which direction the pendulum of his will would swing.

Commanded by God to speak to all the people of Israel, Moses said, "**AND it shall come to pass, if thou shalt hearken**(listen) **diligently unto the voice of the LORD thy God, to observe *and* to do all his commandments which I**(Moses) **command thee this day, that the LORD thy God will set thee on high above all nations of the earth: And all these blessings shall come on thee, and overtake thee, if thou shalt hearken unto the voice of the LORD thy God. Blessed**(abundant) *shalt* **thou** *be* **in the city, and blessed** *shalt* **thou** *be* **in the field. Blessed** *shall be* **the fruit of thy body, and the fruit of thy ground, and the fruit of thy cattle, the increase of thy kine**(cattle), **and the flocks of thy sheep. Blessed** *shall be* **thy basket and thy store. Blessed** *shalt* **thou** *be* **when thou comest in, and blessed** *shalt* **thou** *be* **when thou goest out. The LORD shall cause thine enemies that rise up against thee to be smitten before thy face: they shall come out against thee one way, and flee before thee seven ways. The LORD shall command the blessing upon thee in thy storehouses, and in all that thou settest thine hand unto; and he shall bless thee in the land** which the LORD thy God giveth thee. The LORD shall establish thee an holy people unto himself, as he hath sworn unto thee, if thou shalt keep the commandments of the LORD thy God, and walk in his ways. And all the people(Gentiles) of the earth shall see that thou art called by the name of the LORD; and they shall be afraid of thee. And the LORD shall make thee plenteous in goods, in the fruit of thy body, and in the fruit of thy cattle, and in the fruit of thy ground, in the land which the LORD sware unto thy fathers to give thee. The LORD shall open unto thee his good treasure, the heaven to give the rain unto thy land in his season, and to bless all the work of thine hand: and thou shalt lend unto many nations, and thou shalt not borrow. And the LORD shall make thee the head(leader), and not the tail(follower); and thou shalt be above only, and thou shalt not be beneath; if that thou hearken unto the commandments of the LORD thy God, which I command thee this day, to observe and to do *them:* And thou shalt not go aside from any of the words which I command thee this day, *to* the right hand, or *to* the left, to go after other gods to serve them [Deu. 28:1-14]."

The children of Israel would receive all these blessings as a nation. Individual accolades would become a national collective crown that measured the obedient progress of the nation of Israel. Moses said that they would receive the blessings "**. . . if thou**(the children of Israel) **shalt hearken**(listen) **diligently unto the voice of the LORD thy God, to observe** *and* **to do all his commandments which I command thee this day, that the LORD thy God will set thee on high above all nations of the earth: And all these blessings shall come on thee, and overtake thee, if thou** (as a nation) **shalt hearken unto the voice of the LORD thy God** [Deu. 28:1-2]." These blessings were to be applied nationally according to the conduct of the people of Israel as a whole.

The blessings that the Israelites would receive were abundant and rich. Rich indeed. But not rich at all when compared to the many curses that would come about if they neglected those blessings. The joyous tranquility that the blessings could bring paled in comparison to the misery and anguish that the curses would cause. If they chose to harden their hearts, the nation of Israel would suffer horribly.

If the children of Israel failed to obey the covenant that God had made with them, they would have to face many curses. So that there would not be any surprise by the consequences of their actions, Moses declared the many curses to the children of Israel as a collective nation, saying, "**But it shall come to pass, if thou wilt not hearken**(listen) **unto the voice of the LORD thy God, to observe to do all his commandments and his statutes which I command thee this day; that all these curses shall come upon thee, and overtake thee: Cursed** *shalt* **thou** *be* **in the city, and cursed** *shalt* **thou** *be* **in the field. Cursed** *shall be* **thy basket and thy store. Cursed** *shall be* **the fruit of thy body, and the fruit of thy land, the increase of thy kine, and the flocks of thy sheep. Cursed** *shalt* **thou** *be* **when thou comest in, and cursed** *shalt* **thou** *be* **when thou goest out. The LORD shall send upon thee cursing, vexation, and rebuke, in all that thou settest thine hand unto for to do, until thou be destroyed, and until thou perish quickly; because of the wickedness of thy doings, whereby thou hast forsaken me. The LORD shall make the pestilence**(plague) **cleave unto thee, until he have consumed thee from off the land, whither thou goest to possess it. The LORD shall smite thee with a consumption, and with a fever, and with an inflammation, and with an extreme burning**(fever)**, and with the sword**(war)**, and with blasting**(scorching)**, and with mildew; and they shall pursue thee until thou perish. And thy heaven that** *is* **over thy head shall be brass, and the earth that** *is* **under thee** *shall be* **iron. The LORD shall make the rain of thy land powder and dust: from heaven shall it come down upon thee, until thou be destroyed. The LORD shall cause thee to be smitten before thine enemies: thou shalt go out one way against them, and flee seven ways before them: and shalt be removed into all kingdoms of the earth** [Deu. 28:15-25]." Moses goes on to say, "**The LORD shall bring thee, and thy king which thou shalt set over thee, unto a nation which neither thou nor thy fathers have known; and there shalt thou serve other gods, wood and stone. And thou shalt become an astonishment, a proverb, and a byword, among all nations**(Gentiles) **whither the LORD shall lead thee** [Deu. 28:36-37]."

* * *

Here is where God's truth is beneficial in understanding the application of the blessings and the curses that are written in chapter 28 of the book of Deuteronomy. As the children of the New Testament, we follow the Lord Jesus Christ. The example of Jesus Christ is the foundation of our faith. Jesus Christ should be the first person that we look to for direction. Through the gift of the Holy Ghost, we are joined to the blessed body of believers. The newly generated spiritual nation of God was created through the triumphant testimony of Jesus Christ. Our blessings are defined by that which is within us (Rom. 8:9-11), as opposed to our material abundance that surrounds us (Luke 12:13-15).

Jesus Christ and his apostles were great examples of the blessings and the curses of the New Testament. The blessing of Christ's testimony that God places within our heart and mind gives us the ability to endure in obedience throughout the constant adversity that we face in life (Heb. 12:7). Our Lord was no stranger to this, and Jesus wanted all his followers to know what God expects of us.

Only a few days before he was arrested and crucified, Jesus spoke to his disciples about the tribulation that they were going to face in his absence. In all that Jesus said to them, the most important thing was, **"But he that shall endure unto the end, the same shall be saved** [Mat. 24:13]."

As babes in Christ, most of us are taught that the blessings and the curses of Deuteronomy 28 apply to the Christian body of believers. This instantly takes our focus away from obeying the example of Jesus Christ as our priority. We begin to desire material good fortune above spiritual wisdom. As the children of God, we begin to feel as if we do not deserve to go through trails and distress in the same manner as others who do not acknowledge God.

When we encounter certain situations, if things do not turn out favorably according to the outward appearance, we start to feel that God is against us for one reason or another. We must realize that we are the children of the New Testament, not the children of the Old Testament. First and foremost, we must look forward to the blessing process which takes place within our hearts. It is not the village, the town, the city, the state, or the country that matters. Wherever we dwell on earth, situations will arise to test our faith in Jesus Christ. But through the grace of God, it is not the situation that matters. What matters is what we learn about ourselves because of the situation. Gaining an understanding of God's will through faith that allows us to overcome and endure tribulation and helps us to identify the blessings that have been placed within our hearts: riches that we have received according to the New Testament (Eph. 1:15-23).

According to the Old Testament law, a blessing or a curse could easily be identified by the social standards of the nation of Israel. Jesus introduced a whole new era of blessings and curses from God. It is as simple as this: if we have received the gift of the Holy Ghost from God, then we are blessed in the eyes of God because our situations and our circumstances will no longer define us. Our reaction toward a situation, our behavior during a situation, and our endurance in obedience throughout the situation are what will define us as being blessed, no matter how terrible the outward appearance of any situation may seem to others.

* * *

The blessings and the curses of Deuteronomy 28 should not be associated with those who are saved by the grace of Jesus Christ. In fact, the blessings and the curses of Deuteronomy 28 should not be associated with anyone at all. Keep in mind that Moses is speaking to the children of Israel as a nation.

The Israelites reaped the blessings of Deuteronomy 28 when God allowed them to settle into the land of promise. But according to the words of Moses, if the Israelites chose to disobey God's will, it was said to them, "**And it shall come to pass, *that* as the LORD rejoiced over you to do you good, and to multiply you; so the LORD will rejoice over you to destroy you, and to bring you to nought; and ye shall be plucked from off the land whither**(where) **thou goest to possess it. And the LORD shall scatter thee among all people**(Gentiles)**, from** the one end of the earth even unto the other; and there thou shalt serve other gods, which neither thou nor thy fathers have known, *even* wood and stone. And among these nations(Gentiles) shalt thou find no ease, neither shall the sole of thy foot have rest: but the LORD shall give thee there a trembling heart, and failing of eyes, and sorrow of mind: And thy life shall hang in doubt before thee; and thou shalt fear day and night, and shalt have none assurance of thy life: In the morning thou shalt say, Would(Wish to) God it were even(evening)! and at even thou shalt say, Would(Wish to) God it were morning! for the fear of thine heart wherewith thou shalt fear, and for the sight of thine eyes which thou shalt see** [Deu. 28:63-67]."

All these curses first came on the children of Israel thousands of years ago when Shalmaneser, the king of Assyria, destroyed the northern kingdom of Israel. The destruction of these ten tribes fulfilled the promises of the curses of Deuteronomy 28 for the northern kingdom of Israel. They were removed far from their homeland, and the king of Assyria brought in a mixed multitude of many different nations to dwell there (2 Kings 17).

As for the southern kingdom of Israel, many curses took effect when Nebuchadnezzar, the king of Babylon, came and destroyed Jerusalem, which was the capital city of the southern kingdom of the Israelites (2 Kings 24-25). Just as Deuteronomy 28 states, God scattered the Israelites from one end of the earth even to the other end. The Babylonians and the Assyrians were those fierce nations that came from afar and regarded not the people of old age nor showed favor to those who were young.

Nevertheless, concerning the southern kingdom of Israel, God had mercy on them after being held in captivity for 70 years by the Babylonians and allowed them to return to Jerusalem. In doing so, God also fulfilled the promise that he made to the Israelites in Deuteronomy chapter 30. After pronouncing to the Israelites the many curses that would come on them because of their disobedience, Moses then said to them, "**AND it shall come to pass, when all these things are come upon thee, the blessing and the curse, which I have set before thee, and thou shalt call** *them* **to mind among all the nations**(Gentiles), **whither**(where) **the LORD thy God hath driven thee, And shalt** return unto the LORD thy God, and shalt obey his voice according to all that I command thee this day, thou and thy children, with all thine heart, and with all thy soul; That then the LORD thy God will turn thy captivity, and have compassion upon thee, and will return and gather thee from all the nations, whither the LORD thy God hath scattered thee. If *any* of thine(the Israelites) be driven out unto the outmost *parts* of heaven, from thence(there) will the LORD thy God gather thee, and from thence will he fetch thee: And the LORD thy God will bring thee into the land which thy fathers possessed, and thou shalt possess it; and he will do thee good, and multiply thee above thy fathers [Deu. 30:1-5]."

After the children of Israel remained in Babylon for seventy years, God had mercy on the southern kingdom of Israel and allowed them to return to their home land to rebuild the city of Jerusalem (Jer. 25:8-11 / Ezra 1:1-4). These events show that God was still a part of their lives in a significant way. It was apparent that the blessings and the curses were still much alive within the daily lives of the Israelites who had survived the captivity of Babylon. The Bible shows that the children of Israel continued to be dominated by other kingdoms, even during the ministry of Jesus Christ. According to the authors of the New Testament, the resurrection of Jesus Christ ended the application of the blessings and the curses of Deuteronomy 28.

We are the children of God and brothers and sisters of Jesus Christ according to the New Testament (Heb. 2:11-12). The blessings and the curses of Deuteronomy 28 are now simple reminders of the testimony that God once gave to the Israelites and the consequences of their actions if they failed to obey him. God allowed them to receive the many blessings, although they continually rebelled against him. Therefore, in due time, the consequences of their disobedience resulted in the manifestation of the curses of Deuteronomy 28 when the northern kingdom was destroyed. The book of 2 Kings gives us the details of what took place when the northern kingdom of Israel was destroyed by the Assyrians.

Moreover, the books of 2 Kings, 2 Chronicles, Jeremiah, and Ezekiel all go into detail concerning the events that took place before, during, and after the Babylonians invaded the southern kingdom of Israel. And the books of Ezra and Nehemiah reveal that the Israelites were allowed to return to their homeland after being held captive by the Babylonians for seventy years. But they were still not allowed to independently possess the land. They remained in subjection to the dominating kingdom of the Persians and the Medes.

Why do we need to understand that the blessings and the curses of Deuteronomy 28 were completely done away with by the resurrection of Jesus Christ? Because Jesus Christ himself taught the same thing to the woman that he talked with at the well. While at the well, the woman spoke to Jesus, saying, "**Sir, I perceive that thou art a prophet. Our fathers worshipped in this mountain; and ye say, that in Jerusalem is the place where men ought to worship. Jesus saith unto her, Woman, believe me, the hour cometh, when ye shall neither in this mountain, nor yet at Jerusalem, worship the Father. Ye worship ye know not what: we know what we worship: for salvation is of the Jews. But the hour cometh, and now is, when the true worshippers shall worship the Father in spirit and in truth: for the Father seeketh such to worship him. God *is* a Spirit: and they that worship him must worship *him* in spirit and in truth** [John 4:19-24]." The blessings of Deuteronomy 28 regard the city of Jerusalem as a sacred dwelling place for the people of God, but Jesus said that the city of Jerusalem is not the focus of the New Testament disciples.

Furthermore, the apostles that Jesus Christ sent to spread the gospel also suggested that there was now a heavenly Jerusalem. Paul said within his letter to the Galatians that those who believe in the Old Covenant are in bondage, but those who believe in Jesus Christ now belong to the Jerusalem which is above (Gal. 4:21-26). Also, the author of the letter of Hebrews commented on this subject, saying, "**For ye are not come unto the mount**(mount Horeb) **that might be touched, and that burned with fire. . . . But ye are come unto mount Sion, and unto the city of the living God, the heavenly Jerusalem, and to an innumerable company of angels**(messengers), **To the general assembly and church of the firstborn** . . . [Heb. 12:18,22-23]." And the author of the book of Revelation wrote, saying, "**And I John saw**

the holy city, new Jerusalem, coming down from God out of heaven, prepared as a bride adorned for her husband [Rev. 21:2]." The body of Christ represents the new Jerusalem. The city of God is not a piece of land that exists somewhere on earth for us to go visit and perhaps fight over. If you are saved through grace, you are a member of the city of God.

* * *

It must be noted that there are other chapters within the book of Deuteronomy that contain curses that would apply to an individual separate from the curses of Deuteronomy 28. These curses were to be accounted to individuals independently, due to their own behavior apart from the rest of the nation. In the eyes of the Jewish religious sects, Jesus Christ fell under at least two of these curses as an Israelite who appeared to be committing offenses against the law of Moses.

The Apostle Paul wrote concerning this matter, saying, "**For as many as are of the works of the law**(Old Testament) **are under the curse: for it is written, Cursed** *is* **everyone that continueth not in all things which are written in the book of the law to do them** [Gal. 3:10]." Jesus Christ did not continue in all things that were written in the law of Moses; therefore, the religious elite of his time deemed him to be cursed.

Within Paul's letter to the Galatians, he used the direct quote from Deuteronomy 27:26. Deuteronomy 27:15-26 gives thirteen distinctive things that would deem an individual to be cursed according to their personal behavior. These curses differ from the curses of Deuteronomy 28, in that they were to be applied to a person individually. The words ". . . Cursed *be* he . . ." focuses on the individual person within the context of how Moses introduced these thirteen separate curses.

There are indeed individual curses written within the book of Deuteronomy that would apply to an individual who is subject to the law of Moses regardless if the Israelites remained a nation or not. Although the children of Israel took the land of Canaan by storm, many generations came and passed before they were recognized as a civilized nation rather than a band of tribes dwelling in the land (Judg. 21:25).

For the most part, God tolerated the people's lack of civility for hundreds of years before he allowed the curses of Deuteronomy 28 to overflow as promised.

The blessings of Deuteronomy 28 are recognized all throughout the books of Samuel, Kings, and Chronicles. Once the children of Israel were scattered over the face of the earth due to the destruction of their nation because of these curses, their judicial system then became a religious custom of remembrance to a certain extent.

Before the Assyrians and the Babylonians dismantled their kingdom and occupied their land, the law of Moses was the governing oracle of the nation of Israel regardless of the region in which they were located. When they became captives of another nation, the laws, the judgments, and the statutes became their customary religion (John 19:6-7). The first five books of the Old Testament (Genesis, Exodus, Leviticus, Numbers, and Deuteronomy) were not written specifically for religious purposes. They were written to be the governing system of a nation created by God. When the nation was destroyed and held in captivity, the curses of Deuteronomy 28 revealed themselves (2 Chr. 36:14-18). Regardless of whether the Israelites remained an independent nation or not, there were other blessings and curses written in different parts of the law that continued for all those who still claimed allegiance to the law of God, according to Moses. In pledging allegiance to the law of Moses, the remaining Israelites could continue to claim themselves to be the people of God, even when they did not have a nation to call their own.

With the appearance of Jesus Christ, everything changed. Jesus was born under the law. This is to say that his mother, Mary, and his earthly father, Joseph, were blood descendants of the Israelites. They were Jews according to their observations of the Old Testament customs. Jesus was circumcised eight days after his birth, and his mother offered the sacrifices that included the blood of animals for her purification in remembrance of the Old Testament customs (Luke 2:21-24).

Although Jesus was an Israelite raised as a child in subjection to the moral and religious standards of Moses, when the time of regeneration quickened the spirit of Jesus at about the age of thirty, he stepped forth in the form of rebellion and began to speak many things which seemed contrary to the strict laws of old (Mat. 5:27-45). In this manner, he made himself a curse. For Deuteronomy 27:26 says, "**Cursed *be* he that confirmeth not *all* the words of this** (Old Testament) **law to do them.**"

Our Lord's behavior was most definitely contrary to many aspects of the old law. According to the old law, Jesus became a curse and was hanged on a tree(cross) because of his apparent offenses against the customs of the Israelites. If Jesus Christ was not considered to be an Israelite, he would not have been made subject to ridicule and persecution by the Jewish elders.

The Jews of Christ's era saw him as a deceiver and a blasphemer (Mat. 9:1-3 / John 7:12). For this reason, they declared him to be a curse and requested the Gentile governor Pilate to hang him on a cross. The Jews felt justified in their actions because of Deuteronomy 21:22-23, which says, "**And if a man have committed a sin worthy of death, and he be to be put to death, and thou hang him on a tree: His body shall not remain all night upon the tree, but thou shalt in any wise bury him that day; (for he that is hanged *is* accursed of God;) that thy land be not defiled, which the LORD thy God giveth thee *for* an inheritance.**"

Jesus Christ allowed himself to become a curse according to the old law so that he could become justified as the Messiah according to the new law (Mat. 26:51-54). Paul wrote to the Galatians about Jesus Christ being a curse, saying, "**Christ hath redeemed us from the curse of the law, being made a curse for us: for it is written, Cursed *is* every one that hangeth on a tree: That the blessing of Abraham might come on the Gentiles through Jesus Christ; that we might receive the promise of the Spirit**(Holy Ghost) **through faith** [Gal. 3:13-14]."

Jesus Christ made himself a curse under the Old Testament law for the purpose of abolishing the influence of the Old Testament law concerning all who choose to follow in his footsteps. According to the old law, all those who follow Jesus Christ are also cursed for not abiding by all the things that are written in the old covenant. All those who follow Jesus Christ are also justified according to the new covenant because the example of Jesus Christ is the justification of eternal life.

* * *

The blessings and the curses of Deuteronomy 28 were based solely on abundance and poverty. The Christian faith is designed to eliminate material abundance as the sign of being blessed. The Christian faith is also designed to eliminate material poverty as the sign of being cursed. The blessings and the curses of the New Testament are based solely on internal contentment and happiness, regardless of the abundance of our material goods or even the lack thereof. We are truly cursed if we believe that godliness is gain, and we are truly blessed(happy) when we learn to acknowledge God in all our ways, knowing that the kingdom of heaven is within us (Luke 17:20-21).

When our situations become overwhelming, and we feel that the lack of God's favor towards us is a sign of us somehow being cursed, we must pick up our Bibles and understand that **"BLESSED *is* the man that walketh not in the counsel of the ungodly, nor standeth in the way of sinners, nor sitteth in the seat of the scornful**(boastful)**. But his delight *is* in the law of the LORD; and in his law doth he meditate day and night** [Psa. 1:1-2]." "**Blessed *are* all they that put their trust in him** [Psa. 2:12]." "**BLESSED *is he whose* transgression *is* forgiven, *whose* sin *is* covered. Blessed *is* the man unto whom the LORD imputeth**(account) **not**(no) **iniquity**(perversity)**, and in whose spirit *there* is no guile**(deceit) [Psa. 32:1-2]." "**Blessed *is* that man that maketh the LORD his trust, and respecteth not the proud, nor such as turn aside to lies** [Psa. 40:4]." "**Blessed *is* he that considereth the poor: the LORD will deliver him in time of trouble** [Psa. 41:1]." "**BLESSED *is* the man whom thou chastenest, O LORD, and teachest him out of thy law; That thou mayest give him rest from the days of adversity, until the pit be digged for the wicked** [Psa. 94:12-13]." "**Blessed *are* they that keep judgment, *and* he that doeth righteousness at all times** [Psa. 106:3]." "**Blessed *is* the man *that* feareth the LORD, *that* delighteth greatly in his commandments** [Psa. 112:1]." "**BLESSED *are* the undefiled in the way, who walk in the law of the LORD. Blessed *are* they that keep his testimonies, *and that* seek him with the whole heart** [Psa. 119:1-2]."

Moreover, in the beginning of his ministry Jesus Christ spoke these words to his disciples, saying, "**Blessed *are* the poor**(helpless) **in spirit: for theirs is the kingdom of heaven. Blessed *are* they that mourn: for they shall be comforted. Blessed *are* the meek: for they shall inherit the earth**(world)**. Blessed *are* they which do hunger and thirst after righteousness: for they shall be filled. Blessed *are* the merciful: for they shall obtain mercy. Blessed *are* the pure in heart: for they shall see**(understand) **God**(God's will)**. Blessed *are* the peacemakers: for they shall be called the children of God. Blessed *are* they which are persecuted for righteousness' sake: for theirs is the kingdom of heaven. Blessed are ye, when *men*(*mankind*) shall revile you, and persecute *you*, and shall say all manner of evil against you falsely, for my**(Christ's) **sake** [Mat. 5:3-11]."

By these things, the children of the New Testament know that they are blessed and joyous in the Lord. By these things, the children of the New Testament understand that they are not cursed. If we seek to be justified in God's will according to righteousness, we need not even attempt to measure our spiritual growth by the vain pride of abundance that both the carnal world and the hypocritical religious world have come to acknowledge as being blessed.

No matter what our situation may be, if we are to remain blessed, let us look to Jesus Christ and his apostles and strive to emulate their examples. According to the New Testament, blessings and curses are defined by our ability to remain obedient rather than by our belongings. The blessing and the curses of Deuteronomy 28 cannot be ascribed to the New Testament saints in any way because all those blessings and curses came to an end thousands of years ago. If we desire the blessings described in Deuteronomy 28 to somehow feel comfortable as a child of God, we have apparently taken our eyes off the eternal purpose of God's will for us. Thanks be to God for the blessing of his son Jesus Christ. The blessings and the curses of Deuteronomy 28 have just been revealed in Divine Context.

- -

Context #9 reveals how Satan's destructive behavior is the manifest power of the anger of the LORD.

- -

1 CHRONICLES 21:1-4

1. AND Satan stood up against Israel, and provoked David to number Israel.

2. And David said to Joab(a chief soldier) and to the rulers of the people, Go, number Israel from Beersheba even to Dan; and bring the number of them to me, that I may know *it*.

3. And Joab answered, The LORD make his people an hundred times so many more as they *be:* but, my lord the king, *are* they not all my lord's servants? why then doth my lord require this thing? why will he be a cause of trespass to Israel?

4. Nevertheless the king's word prevailed against Joab.

Satan & The Anger Of The Lord

Divine Context is understanding that the influence of Satan, which provoked David to number the people of Israel, is the direct result of the anger of the LORD.

* * *

Satan has always been the poster child for rebellion, oppression, confusion, destruction, and evil, and rightly so. Satan is a major figure within the Bible. We can be sure that the misinterpretation of the scriptures is where all the reports of Satan's perverted infamy have come from. According to the Bible, Satan is the spiritual influence that represents evil, destruction, and opposition. Satan is also the spiritual influence that represents God's chastisement. Satan, the Devil, the Red Dragon, and the serpent all represent the spirit that opposes truth and torment the hearts and the minds of mankind (Rev. 12:9).

When we think of Satan, the first thing that comes to mind is a caricature with two horns coming out of his forehead and a tail trailing behind him. Many depictions of Satan portray him as being red from head to toe with sharp teeth, pointy ears, and holding a long spear in his hand. As innocent as it may seem, these are the images that have formed our thoughts about what Satan is and what Satan really represents. Satan, better known as the Devil, is the celestial monster that seeks to rob us of our joy and kill all sense of civility within us. As children and young adults, we are taught that God is in a war with Satan and that Jesus Christ came to step in between God and Satan, in order to offer mankind a pathway into God's grace. Many individuals have been called Satan or the Devil in condemnation of their behavior. But after becoming very familiar with the scriptures, what I learned about the relationship between God and Satan settled my thoughts and gave me a clear understanding of the power of God. What if the Bible was to say that Satan is merely a tool for God's anger, a tool for God's wrath, and a tool for God's chastisement?

If it is hard for you to believe that Satan and the anger of the LORD are related, pay close attention to the following scriptures. The author of the book of 1 Chronicles wrote saying, "**AND Satan stood up against Israel, and provoked David to number Israel** [1 Chr. 21:1]." Now, in another portion of the Bible, the author of the book of 2 Samuel spoke of the exact same situation concerning David numbering the children of Israel, saying, "**AND again the anger of the LORD was kindled against Israel, and he**(the anger of the LORD) **moved David against them to say, Go, number Israel and Judah** [2 Sam. 24:1]." Which one is it? Was it the anger of the LORD that moved David to number the people of Israel, or was it Satan that provoked David to number the people of Israel? Are the scriptures letting us know that Satan also represents the anger of the LORD? Let us find out by researching the Bible and doing our best to recognize the operation of Satan's influence on mankind through God's authority.

* * *

God must be in control of all things. It is God who gave Moses the revelation of "The Beginning" in the book of Genesis, and it is God that predicted "The Future" through the Apostle John in the book of Revelation. So, it must be God who is in control of all the things that have transpired and will transpire in between the writings of the books of Genesis and Revelation. The earth rotates nonstop, and we have not found, nor have we heard of any one human being that can stop the earth's rotation or even slow it down. We do not have control over where we are conceived in the womb; in whom or by whom we are conceived; whether we are born male or female; whether we are born black, white, Hispanic, or other; nor are we in control of how short or how tall we will be. All this control belongs to God. He is the LORD of the galaxies, the ruler of the universe, and the master of all things good and bad (Job 12:16 / Pro. 16:4 / Amos 3:6). If God was not in control of all these things, then he could not be self-existing or omnipotent.

As we dissect the scriptures, we will see that Satan is simply a tool that God uses at his own pleasure. Satan is separate from God's righteous will for mankind, but the righteous will for God himself consists of all that God pleases to do. God is God. God makes the rules, God sets the standards, God guides the agenda, and it is God who enforces the laws that he put in place for mankind to abide by. No one can justifiably question God's ways (Job 9:12 / Dan. 4:34-35), because every situation, every scene, everything, and everyone is the clay, and God is the Potter (Rom. 9:18-21).

Satan and all that Satan represents has a purpose. That purpose may be God's chastisement on a certain nation or on certain individuals, so that mortal man can be reminded that we are always subject to the power and grace of God. Satan's purpose may also appear in the form of God's wrath, which is poured out on humans in order to hinder and destroy all chance of hope and dependency on self.

Satan, the Devil, Lucifer, and the serpent are all one in the same. Satan did not create himself. Satan is a product of the authority of the almighty God. Satan is God's belt, God's rod, God's whipping stick, and God's reminder that we are subject to a darkened spirit realm through the curse of Adam's transgression. For this reason, we call on God for protection and pray for peace. God allowed Satan's spiritual influences to lead Adam and Eve astray (Gen. 3:1-6); otherwise, mankind would have never understood the value of having the living God in our lives.

Yes, Satan is God's tool, and God has placed in Satan all that is needed to ruin generations, destroy worlds, and alter desires. For many, to say that God is also in control of Satan would be considered offensive or even malicious. If so, they have never read the Bible with a sincere heart and with an open mind. Life is not an imaginary fairy tale. The power of God, which sustains life and constructs the spiritual character within us, is not a science fiction movie script.

For example, Abimelech, the king of Gerar, wanted to take Abraham's wife Sarah to himself, but God came to him in a dream, saying that he would destroy Abimelech for doing so. Abimelech responded to God by saying, "**Lord, wilt thou slay also a righteous nation? Said he**(Abraham) **not unto me, She *is* my sister? and she, even she herself said, He *is* my brother: in the integrity of my heart and innocency of my hands have I done this. And God said unto him**(Abimelech) **in a dream, Yea, I know that thou didst this in the integrity of thy heart; for I also withheld thee from sinning against me: therefore suffered**(allowed) **I thee not to touch her** [Gen. 20:4-6]."

Who withheld Abimelech from sinning against God? It was God himself. God was in control the whole time. Through the influence of Satan, things may have appeared to be chaotic to Abraham (Gen. 20:10-11), but the purpose was from God. God simply wanted to show Abraham that he would protect him. The only control that Satan has is the control that God allows Satan to have.

If we read the book of Job, we will see that Job did not blame Satan for all the destruction that took away his family, his wealth, and his health. Job took his argument to God. Job debated with his friends about the many things that God allows to happen to the righteous and to the wicked. Satan only has the authority to do what God allows him to do. When Satan presented himself to God, Satan did not ask about Job. It was God that said to Satan, "**Whence**(where) **comest thou? Then Satan answered the LORD, and said, From going to and fro in the earth, and from walking up and down in it. And the LORD said unto Satan, Hast thou considered my servant Job, that *there is* none like him in the earth, a perfect and an upright man, one that feareth God, and escheweth**(shuns) **evil** [Job 1:7-8]?"

Satan was no fool. Satan knew that Job was not in his reach because of the power of God. Therefore, Satan answered the LORD, saying,

"**Doth Job fear God for nought**(nothing)**? Hast not thou made an hedge about him, and about his house, and about all that he hath on every side? thou hast blessed the work of his hands, and his substance is increased in the land. But put forth thine hand**(terror) **now, and touch all that he hath, and he will curse thee to thy face** [Job 1:9-11]."

Satan told God to put forth his power and destroy all that Job had and then see if Job remained faithful to him. Well, how could God put forth his power and touch all that Job had? By giving Satan the authority to do so. In response to Satan, God said, "**Behold, all that he**(Job) **hath *is* in thy power**(dominion)**; only upon himself put not forth thine hand**(power) [Job 1:12]."

God told Satan that he could destroy all that Job had, but he could not harm Job physically, mentally, or spiritually. Eventually, God allowed Satan to harm Job physically as well, but God still did not allow Satan to take away Job's life (Job 2:1-8). In the end, things turned out even better for Job than before. The scars of the terrifying experience that Job endured helped Job appreciate his carnal blessings and respect the power of God so much more.

Before the experience, Job only knew about the power of God. After the experience, Job understood the power of God (Job 42:1-6). Once we learn to accept that Satan is a tool that God used to torment Job for the sake of helping us understand the operation of his power, then many other situations within the Bible will begin to take on a whole new meaning.

* * *

When God revealed to Moses that he was going to kill all the firstborn males of the Egyptians, God said, "**For I will pass through the land of Egypt this night, and will smite**(kill) **all the firstborn in the land of Egypt, both man and beast; and against all the gods of Egypt I will execute judgment: I *am* the LORD. And the blood** (of the Passover lamb) **shall be to you for a token upon the houses where ye *are:* and when I see the blood, I will pass over you, and the plague shall not** be upon you to destroy *you*, when I smite the land of Egypt** [Exo. 12:12-13]."

As we read the scriptures, we can assume that it was God himself that came through Egypt and killed all the firstborn children of the Egyptians. The book of Psalm will show us otherwise. The book of Psalm was written many generations after God delivered the children of Israel from Egypt. Although the book of Psalm is a book of prophecy, it is also filled with the previous experiences of the people of Israel. Therefore, Psalm 78:49-52 says, "**He**(God) **cast upon them**(the Egyptians) **the fierceness of his anger, wrath, and indignation, and trouble, by sending evil angels *among them*. He**(God) **made a way to his anger; he spared not their soul from death, but gave their life over to the pestilence**(plague)**; And smote all the firstborn in Egypt; the chief of *their* strength in the tabernacle of Ham: But made his own people** (the Israelites) **to go forth like sheep, and guided them in the wilderness like a flock.**"

God ordered the hit. God was the power behind all that happened in Egypt on that unforgettable night. It was not as if God lacked the power to stop those evil angels from killing all the firstborn children of the Egyptians. The context of this situation reveals that it was not all about the Egyptians. This was about God revealing himself to the children of Israel in the most memorable way. The living God wanted the Israelites to recognize his power.

* * *

Did Pharaoh, the king of Egypt, harden his own heart and refuse to let the children of Israel depart out of his land? Yes, Pharaoh did harden his heart. Nevertheless, who said that he would harden Pharaoh's heart beforehand? It was God who said to Moses from the very start, "**When thou goest to return into Egypt, see that thou do all those wonders before Pharaoh, which I have put in thine hand: but I will harden his**(Pharaoh's) **heart, that he shall not let the people go** [Exo. 4:21]." Pharaoh did not stand a chance against the power of God. Pharaoh was simply a puppet on a string.

* * *

The prophet Amos spoke to the children of Israel during the reign of Jeroboam, the king of Israel, and during the reign of Uzziah, the king of Judah. Through the prophet Amos, God pronounced destruction on several nations, including the nations of Israel and Judah. Within the midst of all this destruction, God sought for the people of Israel to turn to him. God spoke to the children of Israel through the prophet Amos, saying, "**And I**(God) **also have given you cleanness of teeth in all your cities, and want of bread in all your places: yet have ye not returned unto me, saith the LORD. And also I have withholden the rain from you, when** *there were* **yet three months to the harvest . . . yet have ye not returned unto me, saith the LORD. I have smitten you with blasting and mildew . . . yet have ye not returned unto me, saith the LORD. I have sent among you the pestilence**(plague) **after the manner of Egypt . . . yet have ye not returned unto me, saith the LORD. I have overthrown** *some* **of you, as God overthrew Sodom and Gomorrah, and ye were as a firebrand plucked out of the burning: yet have ye not returned unto me, saith the LORD** [Amos 4:6-11]." God did not do these things to the children of Israel himself. God did these things to the children of Israel by allowing Satan to have the authority to ravage their land and destroy their people.

* * *

The book of Joshua also relates the anger of the LORD to the destruction of the children of Israel. Once Joshua and the armies of the Israelites began to conquer the land that God had promised to give to his people, a few years passed, and things began to settle down. When Joshua was nearing the day of his death, he called all the chief men of Israel to him and reminded them of the testimony of the LORD. Towards the end of Joshua's speech, he spoke to all the elders of the Israelites, saying, "**And, behold, this day I** *am* **going the way of all the earth: and ye know in all your hearts and in all your souls, that not one thing hath failed of all the good things which the LORD your God spake concerning** you; all are come to pass unto you, *and* not one thing hath failed thereof. Therefore it shall come to pass, *that* as all good things are come upon you, which the LORD your God promised you; so shall the LORD bring upon you all evil things, until he have destroyed you from off this good land which the LORD your God hath given you. When ye have transgressed the covenant of the LORD your God, which he commanded you, and have gone and served other gods, and bowed yourselves to them; then shall the anger of the LORD be kindled against you, and ye shall perish quickly from off the good land which he hath given unto you [Jos. 23:14-16]."

* * *

Within the book of Judges, when the children of Israel began to serve the Canaanite gods Baal and Ashtaroth, it is said, "**And the anger of the LORD was hot against Israel, and he(God) delivered them into the hands of spoilers that spoiled them, and he sold them into the hands of their enemies round about, so that they could not any longer stand before their enemies** [Judg. 2:14]." Afterward, God gave his people a leader to deliver them from their enemies, but it was not long thereafter that they fell back into their idolatrous practices and served the gods of the land of Canaan once again. At this time also it is said, "**Therefore the anger of the LORD was hot against Israel, and he(God) sold them into the hand of Chushanrishathaim king of Mesopotamia . . .** [Judg. 3:8]."

* * *

Please know that God is not on the sidelines when tragedy comes our way. Even when we do not know the answer, God knows the answer to the question of "Why?" Within the book of Judges, Abimelech, the son of Gideon, killed seventy men who were his brothers, so that he could become the next Judge over the people of Israel. What did God do three years later? Scripture says, "**Then God sent an evil spirit between Abimelech and the men of Shechem; and the men of Shechem dealt**

treacherously with Abimelech: That the cruelty *done* to the threescore and ten (70) sons of Jerubbaal(Gideon) **might come, and their blood be laid upon Abimelech their brother, which slew**(killed) **them; and upon the men of Shechem, which aided him in the killing of his brethren** [Judg. 9:23-24]." Who sent the evil spirit between Abimelech and the men of Shechem? The scriptures do not say that it was Satan who sent the evil spirit.

* * *

When God anointed David to be king over the children of Israel in place of Saul, what happened when David was anointed with the oil by the prophet Samuel? It is said, "**. . . the Spirit of the LORD came upon David from that day forward. But the Spirit of the LORD departed from Saul, and an evil spirit from the LORD troubled him. And Saul's servants said unto him, Behold now, an evil spirit from God troubleth thee** [1 Sam. 16:13-15]." An evil spirit from who troubled Saul? Yes, an evil spirit from God. Very interesting indeed. But wait, there is even more.

* * *

When Jesus Christ was baptized by John the Baptist, who led Jesus Christ into the wilderness to be tempted by the devil? It was God. The scripture says, "**THEN was Jesus led up of the spirit** (of God) **into the wilderness to be tempted of the devil** [Mat. 4:1]." After battling the influences of the devil for a while, Jesus Christ finally said, "**Get thee hence, Satan: for it is written, Thou shalt worship the Lord thy God, and him only shalt thou serve** [Mat. 4:10]." God allowed Satan to become a tool to test Jesus Christ and bring the evidence of Christ's anointing to the forefront. This spiritual battle did not take place in the presence of others. This spiritual battle between Jesus and Satan took place when Jesus was alone in the wilderness. This battle was meant to strengthen Jesus so that he could gain the experience to teach his followers how to resist Satan.

* * *

The anger of the LORD is no doubt the power of Satan at its fullest. When Moses was about to go onto the mountain and surrender his life to God, God forewarned Moses about how his anger would eventually come on the children of Israel. The people of Israel had not even stepped one foot into the promised land, but God felt that it was necessary to reveal this to Moses, saying, "**Behold, thou shalt sleep with thy fathers; and this people will rise up, and go a whoring after the gods of the strangers of the land, whither they go *to be* among them, and will forsake me, and break my covenant which I have made with them. Then my anger shall be kindled against them in that day, and I will forsake them, and I will hide my face**(presence) **from them, and they shall be devoured, and many evils and troubles shall befall them; so that they will say in that day, Are not these evils come upon us, because our God *is* not among us** [Deu. 31:16-17]?" Satan was already on standby to do what he was designed to do. All Satan needed was the liberty to fulfill what was already spoken by God.

* * *

Within the Old Testament, there are many examples of the anger of the LORD being kindled against his people. When Achan and Zabdi of the tribe of Judah took forbidden items from Jericho when the wall fell, it was the anger of the LORD that was kindled against them (Jos. 7:1,25-26). When David attempted to bring the ark of the covenant into Jerusalem, and Uzzah touched the ark because it seemed as if the ark was going to fall off the cart, it was the anger of the LORD that was kindled against Uzzah (2 Sam. 6:7). When God was upset with Jehu the king of Israel and delivered them into the power of the king of Syria, it was the anger of the LORD that was kindled against Israel (2 Kings 13:3). And when David numbered the children of Israel, the result of David's actions led to God allowing the angel of the LORD to kill at least seventy thousand men (2 Sam. 24:15 / 1 Chr. 21:14-15).

* * *

Furthermore, when Jesus Christ was in the temple disputing with the Jews about their origins, Jesus Christ said to them, "**Why do ye not understand my speech?** *even* **because ye cannot hear my word. Ye are of** *your* **father the devil, and the lusts of your father ye will do. He was a murderer from the beginning, and abode not in the truth, because there is no truth in him. When he speaketh a lie, he speaketh of his own: for he is a liar, and the father of it** [John 8:43-44]." Jesus said that the devil is the father of lies. Once again, we know that the word "devil" is just another title used to describe Satan.

As we read the book of 1 Kings, we will come across something very interesting in chapter 22. Jehoshaphat, who was the king of Judah, had joined up with Jezebel's husband, Ahab, the king of Israel, to go and fight against the king of Syria for the city of Ramoth. As all the false prophets of Jezebel started declaring victory before the fighting even started, the king of Judah wanted to hear from a more reliable source: a prophet of the LORD. Therefore, they sent for a prophet of the LORD named Micaiah. When Micaiah began to speak, he said to the two kings, "**I saw the LORD sitting on his throne, and all the host of heaven standing by him on his right hand and on his left. And the LORD said, Who shall persuade Ahab, that he may go up and fall at Ramoth-gilead? And one said on this manner, and another said on that manner. And there came forth a spirit, and stood before the LORD, and said, I will persuade him. And the LORD said unto him**(the spirit), **Wherewith? And he**(the spirit) **said, I will go forth, and I will be a lying spirit in the mouth of all his prophets. And he**(God) **said, Thou shalt persuade** *him,* **and prevail also: go forth, and do so. Now therefore, behold, the LORD hath put a lying spirit in the mouth of all these thy prophets, and the LORD hath spoken evil concerning thee** [1 Kings 22:19-23]."

There is no doubting what you just read. Yes, God sent a lying spirit, which filled the hearts of all the false prophets of Jezebel. Those prophets persuaded Jezebel's husband, Ahab, the king of Israel, to go into battle and face his death. Although the devil is the father of lies, who did the lying spirit have to get permission from before it could influence the false prophets of Israel? It had to get its orders from God. And it's not just the fact that the lying spirit was sent from God, but God also spoke concerning the power of the lying spirit, saying, "**Thou shalt persuade him**(*Ahab*)**, and prevail also** . . . [1 Kings 22:22]." The lying spirit could not fail because it was ordained by God to succeed.

* * *

The Apostle Paul was also affected by Satan. The context of Paul's situation is speaking in terms of glorying in our infirmities, as opposed to boasting about our achievements according to our works in the Lord. While referring to those who thought that they were all high and mighty in the Corinthian church, Paul wrote to them saying, "**For though I would desire to glory, I shall not be a fool; for I will say the truth: but *now* I forbear, lest any man should think of me above that which he seeth me *to be*, or *that* he heareth of me. And lest I should be exalted above measure through the abundance of the revelations, there was given to me a thorn**(annoyance) **in the flesh, the messenger of Satan to buffet me, lest I should be exalted above measure. For this thing I besought the Lord thrice**(three times)**, that it might depart from me. And he said unto me, My grace is sufficient for thee: for my strength is made perfect in weakness**(neglecting of self)**. Most gladly therefore will I rather glory in my infirmities, that the power of Christ may rest upon me** [2 Cor 12:6-9]." Instead of removing Satan's annoyance from Paul, God allowed it to remain, and evidently, God gave Paul the ability to endure, proving that the anointing of Jesus Christ abides within Paul.

* * *

God's throne is not magnificent because it is filled with priceless rubies and stones. Nor is God's throne mighty because it is built and overlaid with the finest natural materials and precious minerals known to man. God's throne, which is God's word, is magnificent because it sits above the galaxies directing the traffic of the universe so that you and I can look to him and acknowledge that God is everything that anything has something to do with (Isa. 45:7).

Orchestrating the planets and the stars that fill our solar system is all in a day's work for God. Directing the traffic of human life is like a walk in the park for our father. Those things that may seem tragic and awful now hold much more weight of glory in the time to come. The signal lights of our lives will not turn green, yellow, or red without the influence of God. Our God is the offense and the defense. Why? Because he is God.

As we come to God, we must come to God for truth and not for selective enlightenment. We must read God's word with an open mind and not attempt to twist God's word to please our own mental conceptions of who we think God should be. If we come to God sincerely seeking to build a relationship with him through the truth of his word, we will then see that God is who we shall turn to in times of comfort and discomfort.

God's authority and God's power is not what we think it is. God's authority and God's power is what it is. God is the God within the scriptures. The living God in whom we should believe in is not the god of our story book imaginations.

This Divine Context was not written to confuse anyone's thoughts of God's glory, God's mercy, God's goodness, or God's righteousness. The sole purpose of these words is to inform everyone who thinks that Satan is somehow running things that he is not. Once again, Satan is a tool of God's wrath, a tool of God's anger, and a tool of God's chastisement. In many instances throughout the Bible, Satan is used to execute God's wrathful anger (2 Kings 17:17-18). However, there are also many places within the Bible when Satan is used as a tool to chastise and correct those who are in God's grace, so that they could remain humble and continue to allow themselves to be conformed into the image of God's sincere will (Luke 22:31-32 / Rom. 16:17-20 / 1 Cor. 5:1-5 / 2 Cor. 12:6-9 / Heb. 12:5-8 / 1 Pet. 5.8-10). Let us pray that we fall on the chastisement side of the authority that Satan is allowed to have through the power of God. Because then, at least, we know that comfort will follow the lessons learned.

Satan and the anger of the LORD are related to one another. To deny this fact is to deny the truth of the Bible. As we accept God, we must understand that God is a God of judgment, and all things are subject to be used in the execution of his judgment. Whether those things be angels of darkness or angels of light, they are all under the authority of God's power.

I was once told a small tale about the heartache and pain that Satan experiences. This made me laugh when I thought about the accuracy of it. One day Satan was sitting outside of a church crying. When church service was over, the members came out and were shocked to see Satan with his eyes full of tears. After watching Satan for a while, they finally said, "Satan, why are you outside of this church crying?" Satan gathered himself and looked around at the congregation. Satan then said, "All through the week I go through this, and especially on Sundays. You all talk about me and slander my name on every corner. I get blamed for every sickness, every sad moment, and every destructive act that happens to you people. I think it is about time for you all to start blaming God for some of these things."

This fictitious tale of Satan reminds me of Job's experience. Job's example teaches us not to concentrate so much on the influences of Satan, but rather, we must focus all of our attention on the authority of God and on the ways of God. For if we seek truth, God himself is the source of all that we will learn concerning the ups and the downs of life. Listen to the famous words that Job spoke to his wife as she insisted that Job should curse God and die.

Although Job was hurting and sad because of all that had happened to him, Job did not hesitate to tell his wife that she was speaking foolishly. Then Job asked his wife this question, **"What? shall we receive good at the hand**(power) **of God, and shall we not receive evil** [Job 2:10]**?"** Job got it, and for a moment, Job was willing to accept that all power belonged to God, even though his world had been turned upside down. Have mercy on us all, O LORD, for your power, your ways, and your authority over our lives are often too much for us to understand. Satan and the anger of the LORD have just been revealed in Divine Context.

Context #10 reveals that despite the wickedness of the evil Queen Jezebel, she was not a whore.

1 KINGS 16:28-31

28. So Omri slept with his fathers, and was buried in Samaria: and Ahab his son reigned in his stead(place).

29. And in the thirty and eighth year of Asa king of Judah began Ahab the son of Omri to reign over Israel: and Ahab the son of Omri reigned over Israel in Samaria twenty and two years.

30. And Ahab the son of Omri did evil in the sight of the LORD above all that *were* before him.

31. And it came to pass, as if it had been a light thing for him to walk in the sins of Jeroboam the son of Nebat, that he took to wife Jezebel the daughter of Ethbaal king of the Zidonians, and went and served Baal, and worshiped him(Baal).

Jezebel Was Not A Whore

Divine Context is understanding that Jezebel was not a whore, although she did influence the children of Israel to commit idolatry(whoredom) by serving her native god Baal, which was an abomination in the sight of the God of Israel.

* * *

The Jezebel of myth and the Jezebel of the Bible bears two totally different characteristics. The myth of Jezebel tells us that she is a lustful spirit that enters local congregations with the intention of enticing members to partake in rebellion and sexual misconduct by any means necessary. It is thought that the spirit of Jezebel entices all men and women to commit fornication and, in many cases, even adultery. The Jezebel that we have been taught is not a family-oriented woman at all. If a woman who has any children of her own is branded with the title of being a Jezebel, it would be assumed that her children are neglected by her because of her lack of respect for herself.

The myth of Jezebel directs our minds to believe that faithfulness is something not to be considered when thinking of Jezebel and that her goal is to dominate men and ruin families for the sake of satisfying her own lustful desire. She frequents the churches and the religious gatherings in search of her prey. She swings her hips from side to side when she walks, sending out her mating call to men of all races, young and old.

Once a Jezebel takes hold of you, there is no escaping her grip. Though you may desire to make Jezebel all yours, she will never be faithful to any one man. Jezebel belongs to all men and women. Everyone who crosses her path receives an invite to moral corruption. A church house prostitute is what they call Jezebel. A whore is what Jezebel is thought to be. Jezebel represents a no-good female dog. She is the half-naked woman on the street corners and within the church houses who seeks to have her way with all those of influence who enter her presence. This is the mythical Jezebel that mankind has declared throughout history.

The Jezebel that embodies the subject matter of confused conversations is a product of our imagination or ignorance. Jezebel's mythical reputation perhaps comes from those who did not understand the heavenly context of Revelation 2:18-29. Nevertheless, the true context of Jezebel's life and death is preserved within the Old Testament books of the kings of Israel.

* * *

Because of the sins of king Solomon, God separated ten tribes from the sons of David and appointed Jeroboam of the tribe of Ephraim to be the king over those ten tribes (1 Kings 11:26-36). The tribe of Judah and the tribe of Benjamin were both left in place for David's sons to rule because God promised David that he would always have a son to rule over his people. The ten tribes became known as the kingdom of Israel, while the tribes of Judah and Benjamin became known as the kingdom of Judah. Omri, the sixth king of Israel, chose the city of Samaria to be the capital city of these ten tribes. Omri was the king in Samaria for twelve years. When Omri died, his son Ahab then became the king of Israel and chose a Zidonian woman by the name of Jezebel to be his wife.

Choosing a woman of another nation was a direct transgression of God's law. Before the children of Israel entered the land of promise, Moses warned them not to mingle with the other nations, saying, "**. . . Neither shalt thou make marriages with them; thy daughter**

thou shalt not give unto his son, nor his daughter shalt thou take unto thy son. For they will turn away thy son from following me, that they may serve other gods: so will the anger of the LORD be kindled against you, and destroy thee suddenly [Deu. 7:3-4]."

Ahab, the seventh king of the northern kingdom of Israel, was not the first to transgress the law of God by marrying a woman of another nation. It became a common practice among the people of Israel to disregard the law of God. When Ahab married Jezebel, he not only added more evil to his deeds in the eyes of the LORD, but he also introduced a queen to God's people who cared nothing for the traditional law of God.

The Bible first mentions the city of Sidon in Genesis 10:19 as a border city of the Canaanites. Sidon and Zidon are the same place. The lord of the Canaanite religion was Baal (Judg. 2:8-13). Baal was worshiped as the fertility god. Jezebel used her authority as the queen of Israel to flood the northern kingdom with Baal worship.

A prophet of God by the name of Elijah was the chief prophet during the reign of Ahab. Through God, Elijah cursed the land and pronounced a famine in it. Ahab and his servants searched tirelessly for Elijah, but they could not find him. After three years, Elijah finally showed himself to one of the king's servants named Obadiah, who was both afraid and relieved to see Elijah. The harm that Jezebel had caused to the prophets of the LORD is evident in how Obadiah responded to Elijah, saying, "**Was it not told my lord** (Elijah) **what I did when Jezebel slew**(killed) **the prophets of the LORD, how I hid an hundred men of the LORD's prophets by fifty in a cave, and fed them with bread and water** [1 Kings 18:13]?" Jezebel had set out to destroy all of God's prophets and replace them with the prophets who worshiped Baal.

When king Ahab and Elijah entered one another's presence, an argument over who was doing the most harm to the kingdom ensued. The first thing that Ahab said to Elijah was, "*Art* **thou he that troubleth Israel** [1 Kings 18:17]?" Elijah then answered Ahab, saying, "**I have not troubled Israel; but thou, and thy father's house, in that ye have forsaken the commandments of the LORD, and thou hast followed Baalim**(a false god). **Now therefore send,** *and* **gather to me all Israel unto mount Carmel, and the prophets of Baal four hundred and**

fifty, and the prophets of the groves four hundred, which eat at Jezebel's table [1 Kings 18:18-19]."

Elijah then went about to prove to all the people that the God of Israel was the one and only living God. While on Mount Carmel, Elijah said to the people of Israel, "**How long halt ye between two opinions? if the LORD *be* God, follow him: but if Baal, *then* follow him** [1 Kings 18:21]." It was Elijah himself against eight hundred and fifty prophets of Baal. Both Elijah and the eight hundred and fifty prophets offered a burnt sacrifice. The prophets of Jezebel offered their sacrifice to Baal, and Elijah offered his sacrifice to the true God of Israel. The prophets of Baal were there all day yelling and cutting themselves, but Baal never responded. Elijah began to mock the prophets of Jezebel, saying, "**Cry aloud: for he**(Baal) ***is* a god; either he is talking, or he is pursuing, or he is in a journey, *or* peradventure**(perhaps) **he sleepeth, and must be awaked** [1 Kings 18:27]."

At the time of the customary evening offering, Elijah repaired the altar of the LORD that the prophets of Baal had broken down. He then put the wood in order on the altar and cut the bull into its proper pieces according to the commandments of the LORD. Elijah was so sure of the LORD that he poured twelve barrels of water on the sacrifice. As Elijah prayed to God, fire came down and consumed everything: the wood, the water, the stones of the altar, the dust, and the sacrifice. All the people that witnessed this bowed their heads to the ground and confessed, "**The LORD, he *is* the God; the LORD, he *is* the God** [1 Kings 18:39]." Then Elijah took all the prophets of Jezebel and killed them. Elijah prayed to the LORD, and after three long years of famine, God allowed it to rain once again in Samaria.

Ahab returned home and told his wife Jezebel what Elijah had done to all her prophets. Jezebel, in her anger, "**. . . sent a messenger unto Elijah, saying, So let the gods do *to me,* and more also, if I make not thy life as the life of one of them**(her prophets) **by to morrow about this time** [1 Kings 19:2]." Fearing for his life, Elijah fled and went to a place called Beersheba.

Once things settled down in Samaria, king Ahab went down to a place named Jezreel and asked a man named Naboth if he could buy his vineyard. The vineyard was an inheritance of Naboth's father, so Naboth refused to sell it to the king. Ahab then returned home and sat around looking sad because Naboth refused to sell him the vineyard. When his wife Jezebel saw this, she asked Ahab, "**Dost thou now govern the kingdom of Israel? arise, *and* eat bread, and let thine heart be merry: I will give thee the vineyard of Naboth the Jezreelite** [1 Kings 21:7]."

Jezebel then sent letters to the elders of Naboth's city, saying, "**Proclaim a fast, and set Naboth on high among the people: And set two men, sons of Belial**(wickedness)**, before him, to bear witness against him, saying, Thou didst blaspheme God and the king. And *then* carry him out, and stone him, that he may die** [1 Kings 21:9-10]." The death letters of Jezebel were written in king Ahab's name and sealed with the king's signet. The men of Jezreel thought that they were following the directions of the king as they formed a plan to kill Naboth.

The elders and the nobles of Jezreel took Naboth and stoned him, killing him as Jezebel desired. When king Ahab heard that Naboth was dead, he then went and took possession of Naboth's vineyard. Through the wickedness of his wife, Jezebel, Ahab finally got what he wanted. Jezebel cared for the king, but this was not the kind of care that the God of Israel justified.

Ahab wanted Naboth's vineyard, but according to scripture, it seems as if the king was not willing to do anything drastic in order to acquire it. He was going to wallow in his sadness for a while and accept that according to the laws of Israel, Naboth had the right to keep hold of his father's inheritance (Deu. 19:14).

Jezebel, on the other hand, cared nothing for the long-held traditions of Israel concerning inheritance. Her husband was the king, he wanted that vineyard, and in her eyes, whatever she had to do for the king to have it, she would make it happen. Does this sound like an unfaithful spouse? I think not. It sounds as if Jezebel was a dangerously faithful spouse to her husband, Ahab.

God recognized the maliciousness of Jezebel in how she had Naboth killed just to obtain his vineyard for the king. Thinking that everything was fine, Ahab and Jezebel went about with their lives like nothing out of the ordinary had taken place. Therefore, the LORD sent word to Elijah, saying, "**Arise, go down to meet Ahab king of Israel, which *is* in Samaria: behold, *he is* in the vineyard of Naboth, whither**(where) **he is gone down to possess it. And thou shalt speak unto him, saying, Thus saith the LORD, Hast thou killed, and also taken possession? . . . Thus saith the LORD, In the place where dogs licked the blood of Naboth shall dogs lick thy blood, even thine** [1 Kings 21:18-19]." Ahab then responded to Elijah by saying, "**Hath thou found me, O mine enemy? And he**(Elijah) **answered, I have found *thee:* because thou hast sold thyself to work evil in the sight of the LORD. Behold, I**(the LORD) **will bring evil upon thee, and will take away thy posterity**(descendants)**, and will cut off from Ahab him that pisseth against the wall, and him that is shut up and left in Israel, And will make thine house like the house of Jeroboam** (1 Kings 15:25-30) **the son of Nebat, and like the house of Baasha** (1 Kings 16:8-13) **the son of Ahijah, for the provocation wherewith thou hast provoked *me* to anger, and made Israel to sin. And of Jezebel also spake the LORD, saying, The dogs shall eat Jezebel by the wall of Jezreel. Him that dieth of Ahab in the city the dogs shall eat; and him that dieth in the field shall the fowls of the air eat** [1 Kings 21:20-24]."

* * *

Eventually, king Ahab died, and many years came and went before Jezebel would reap what she had sown. It was not until God used the prophet Elisha to anoint Jehu king over Israel that the actions of Jezebel would come back to haunt her. Elisha was the understudy of the prophet Elijah. When Elijah's ministry ended, Elisha replaced Elijah as the chief prophet in the kingdom of Israel (2 Kings 2:9-15). Elisha sent one of his students to a place named Ramoth-Gilead to anoint Jehu and proclaim that Jehu was now the king of Israel in Samaria. When the prophet found Jehu, he said, "**Thus saith the LORD God of Israel, I have anointed thee king over the people of the LORD, *even* over Israel. And thou shalt smite the house of Ahab thy master, that I may** avenge the blood of my servants the prophets, and the blood of all the servants of the LORD, at the hand of Jezebel [2 Kings 9:6-7]."

At this time, Ahaziah had become the king of Judah in Jerusalem, and Jehoram, the stepson of Ahab, was the king of Israel in Samaria because Ahab had no sons. Nevertheless, Jezebel remained the queen of Israel. Jehoram, king of Samaria, and Ahaziah king of Judah, were very fond of one another. When Jehoram was wounded in battle with the Syrians, he went to recover from his injuries in Jezreel. Ahaziah, the king of Judah, decided to come to Jezreel and visit Jehoram. Neither Jehoram nor Ahaziah knew that Jehu had been anointed king over Israel by the LORD, or that Jehu was commanded to execute vengeance on the house of Ahab because of the wickedness of his wife, Jezebel.

As Ahaziah and Jehoram were in Jezreel relaxing, Jehu came near with his soldiers, that were gathered around him. After Jehu ignored the messengers that Jehoram sent to greet him, Jehoram and Ahaziah decided to go out and meet Jehu for themselves. When Jehoram came to Jehu, he said, "*Is it* **peace, Jehu** [2 Kings 9:22]**?**" Jehu then answered Jehoram saying, "**What peace, so long as the whoredoms**(idolatry) **of thy mother Jezebel and her witchcrafts** *are so* **many? And Joram**(Jehoram) **turned his hands, and fled, and said to Ahaziah,** *There is* **treachery, O Ahaziah. And Jehu drew a bow with his full strength, and smote**(hit) **Jehoram between his arms, and the arrow went out at his heart, and he sunk down in his chariot** [2 Kings 9:22-24]."

After Jehu killed both Jehoram, the king of Israel, and Ahaziah, the king of Judah, Jehu proceeded to the king's palace in Jezreel to confront Jezebel. The scripture then says, "**And when Jehu was come to Jezreel, Jezebel heard** *of it;* **and she painted her face, and tired**(made better) **her head**(hair)**, and looked out at a window. And as Jehu entered in at the gate, she said,** *Had* **Zimri peace, who slew**(killed) **his master? And he lifted up his face to the window, and said, Who** *is* **on my side? who? And there looked out to him two** *or* **three eunuchs. And he said, Throw her down. So they threw her down: and** *some* **of her blood was sprinkled on the wall, and on the horses: and he**

trode(trampled) **her under foot. And when he was come in, he did eat and drink, and said, Go, see now this cursed *woman*, and bury her: for she *is* a king's daughter. And they went to bury her: but they found no more of her than the skull, and the feet, and the palms of *her* hands** [2 Kings 9:30-35]." This concludes the documented life and death of Jezebel, the wicked queen of Israel.

* * *

What part of Jezebel's life suggests that Jezebel was a prostitute or a whore who seduced men by presenting herself as a sexual playmate? Was it when Jehu was about to kill Jezebel's son Jehoram, and Jehoram asked Jehu, "***Is it* peace, Jehu?**" And Jehu answered, "**What peace, so long as the whoredoms of thy mother Jezebel and her witchcrafts *are so* many** [2 Kings 9:22]?"

The word "whoredoms" spoken by Jehu does not suggest that Jezebel was a whore in a sexual manner. Jehu also mentioned the witchcraft of Jezebel along with her whoredoms. Jezebel's whoredoms and witchcrafts were in reference to her idol worship of the Canaanite god Baal. These words by Jehu had nothing to do with Jezebel herself having sexual escapades of any kind. Jezebel's whoredoms represent idolatry, not adultery, as if she had been unfaithful to her husband, king Ahab.

In order to justify the misconception that Jezebel was a whore, some may even turn to the portion of the scripture that says, "**. . . she painted her face, and tired**(made better) **her head**(hair)**, and looked out at the window** [2 Kings 9:30]." This mistake can arise when we compare Jezebel's situation to certain words written within the book of Proverbs.

Within chapter 7 of the book of Proverbs, there is a parable that says, "**Say unto wisdom, Thou *art* my sister; and call understanding *thy* kinswoman: That they may keep thee from the strange woman, from the stranger *which* flattereth with her words. For at the window of my house I looked through my casement**(window frame)**, And beheld among the simple ones, I discerned among the youth, a young man void of understanding, Passing through the street near her corner; and he went the way to her house, In the twilight, in the** evening, in the black and dark night: And behold, there met him a woman *with* the attire of an harlot(whore), and subtil of heart. (She *is* loud and stubborn; her feet abide not in her house: Now *is* she without, now in the streets, and lieth in wait at every corner.) So she caught him, and kissed him, *and* with an impudent(bold) face said unto him, *I have* peace offerings with me; this day have I payed my vows. Therefore came I forth to meet thee, diligently to seek thy face, and I have found thee. I have decked my bed with coverings of tapestry, with carved *works,* with fine linen of Egypt(bondage). I have perfumed my bed with myrrh, aloes, and cinnamon. Come, let us take our fill of love until the morning: let us solace ourselves with loves. For the goodman *is* not at home, he is gone a long journey: He hath taken a bag of money with him, *and* will come home at the day appointed. With her much fair speech she caused him to yield, with the flattering of her lips she forced him. He goeth after her straightway, as an ox goeth to the slaughter, or as a fool to the correction of the stocks; Till a dart strike through his liver; as a bird hasteth to the snare, and knoweth not that it *is* for his life. Hearken(listen) unto me now therefore, O ye children, and attend to the words of my mouth. Let not thine heart decline to her ways, go not astray in her paths. For she hath cast down many wounded: yea, many strong *men* have been slain by her. Her house *is* the way to hell, going down to the chambers of death [Pro. 7:4-27]."

This parable in the book of Proverbs has nothing at all to do with Jezebel, the queen of Israel. The fact that Jezebel cleaned herself up and looked down out of a window to Jehu does not suggest that she was trying to seduce Jehu sexually. If this is one's interpretation of the situation between Jehu and Jezebel, hopefully, they will read the scriptures once again and pay close attention to what Jezebel said to Jehu when she saw him through the window. Jezebel looked down to Jehu and said to him, "*Had* Zimri peace, who slew his master [2 Kings 9:31]?"

The words that Jezebel spoke to Jehu were about the deeds of Zimri, the servant of Elah, the former king of Israel. Zimri conspired against king Elah and killed him. Then Zimri attempted to reign over Israel in Elah's place. Zimri destroyed all of Elah's family just as Jehu was attempting to do to Ahab's family, including Jezebel. Zimri only remained a self-anointed king over Israel for seven days. The reason Zimri's reign only lasted for one week was that when the people of Israel heard that Zimri had killed Elah, rather than embrace Zimri as their king, the people went out and made Omri, Jezebel's father-in-law, the king instead of Zimri (1 Kings 16:8-16). When Zimri saw this, the scripture says that "... he(Zimri) **went into the palace of the king's house, and burnt the king's house over him with fire, and died** ... [1 Kings 16:18]." Jezebel did not know that Jehu was truly anointed by God to be king over the northern kingdom of Israel. Jezebel thought that Jehu had self-appointed himself to be king, just like Zimri did. This is the reason why Jezebel questioned Jehu, asking if Zimri found peace after he murdered a king of Israel.

The reason why Jezebel took the time to make her appearance look better by painting her face and beautifying her hair when she heard that Jehu had come was that she was the queen of the kingdom of Israel. Hearing how Jehu had murdered her son Jehoram, the king, she knew that her influence on the kingdom would now come to an end. Knowing that the person who just killed her son had come to the king's palace, Jezebel simply made herself look more presentable as someone of royalty most certainly would, hoping that Jehu would recognize her stature in the kingdom and somehow find it in his heart to spare her life. However, Jezebel's stature in the kingdom was the reason Jehu had come to take her life in the first place. Nevertheless, the situation itself does not bear a hint of a sexual invitation to Jehu by Jezebel.

Jezebel was not a weak and feeble queen. She was a murderer, a cold-blooded killer. She was strong, she was proud, and she was accustomed to imposing her will on whoever stood in her way. She was not going to let a mere servant like Jehu see her sweat. She was going to at least appear strong and confident, holding on to the hope that her status in the kingdom would give her a chance to save her own life.

* * *

According to the documented testimony of Jezebel's life, we cannot say that Jezebel was a whore who betrayed her husband and slept with other men. The strange woman with the attire of a harlot spoken of in the book of Proverbs has nothing to do with Jezebel in the literal sense. Jezebel was not a whore, nor was Jezebel a prostitute. Jezebel did not appear half-naked during religious ceremonies to share sexual intercourse with numerous men.

If we read the book of Revelation, we can perhaps get a glimpse into why so many people throughout history have also tagged Jezebel with the title of being a whore. We must be warned, though, that many of the words written within the book of Revelation should not be taken literally. Remember this!

The book of Revelation is the last book of the Bible. It is a book that contains parables and metaphors that can easily escape the grasp of our mental comprehension unless spiritual discernment is implemented in order to open and reveal the mysterious wisdom of God.

The book of Revelation is certainly not a book that we should read in the literal sense for the most part. Yes, there are literal things and events that occur therein, but the literal events are mere specks when compared to the metaphorical contents of all that is proclaimed within it. Revelation is a book of the Bible that is arguably one of the chief culprits of our misinterpretation of God's word. This book is the finest example of not always saying what it is saying.

When the spirit of Christ spoke to the body of believers in the church of Thyatira, he said, "**I know thy works, and charity, and service, and faith, and thy patience, and thy works; and the last *to be* more than the first. Notwithsanding I have a few things against thee, because thou sufferest**(allow) **that woman Jezebel, which calleth herself a prophetess, to teach and to seduce my servants to commit fornication, and to eat things sacrificed unto idols. And I gave her space to repent of her fornication; and she repented not. Behold, I will cast her into a bed, and them that commit adultery with her into great tribulation, except they repent of their deeds. And I will kill her children with death**(ignorance)**; and all the churches shall know that I am he which searcheth the reins and**

hearts: and I will give unto every one of you according to your works [Rev. 2:19-23]."

As we read words such as "fornication," "adultery," "seduce," and "bed," our thoughts automatically suggest that the scriptures are speaking of some form of sexual activity. When context is applied, we will understand that such words hold much more meaning than that of our sensual minds.

The book of Revelation says that the woman Jezebel calls herself a prophetess. We all know that the real Jezebel died long ago, even hundreds of years before the book of Revelation was written. This Jezebel of the New Testament is the manifest characteristics of the false church, the fictitious bride of Christ, the collective body of the hypocritical believers in Jesus Christ who claim unity with the faithful and obedient lovers of the Lord (1 Cor. 1:11-13 / Phi. 1:12-17/3:17-19 / 2 Pet. 2:1-3 / Jude 1:10-13).

The Jezebel of the New Testament represents those who teach individuals that it is a righteous thing to accept Jesus Christ without making a wholehearted commitment to becoming one with God's new covenant. In doing so, this Jezebel displays the example of the fornication that the book of Revelation is speaking of. Partaking in the functions that recognize God and Jesus Christ but not putting forth the sincere effort to commit to the responsibilities that are needed to become one with God's will, is an example of spiritual fornication (1 Cor. 5:1).

When we read 1 Corinthians 5:1, the scripture focuses on a form of fornication rather than literal adultery, although it speaks of someone having their father's wife. Believers are the bride of Christ (2 Cor. 11:2). When we fellowship with the members of the body of Christ, all members should be committed to becoming one with the example of Jesus Christ and his Apostles. Spiritual fornicators refuse to sincerely make a commitment to become one with God's will. Although they partake in many traditional Christian activities, such as attending church and acknowledging that Jesus is real, they continue to practice a sinful life. This is the example of the " **. . . old leaven . . .** " that Paul is speaking of in 1 Corinthians 5:7-8.

The Jezebel of the New Testament is the collective body of those who introduce lies and man-made traditions to the servants of Jesus Christ, teaching them that it is acceptable to live a sinful life and accept their man-made teachings while belonging to the Christian faith. This is idolatry and witchcraft in the form of doctrines, titles, and denominational organizations of men and women who claim allegiance to the righteousness of Jesus Christ (Gal. 5:19-21), but they only seek to fulfill the will of their own historical organizations and traditions.

Most of the New Testament generation think that an idol is a molten image of some type of figurine. In most cases, this is true, but when it comes to the detailed will of God, according to the New Testament, an idol is something or someone that we put before God's righteousness. The book of Revelation does not focus on the idol itself, but rather it focuses on things that are offered in sacrifice to idols.

In the case of many religious sects and denominations that claim to be a part of the Christian belief, their efforts in worshiping God are directed more towards their doctrines than the example of Jesus Christ. Their doctrines and traditions are their idols. And their efforts to follow their own doctrines and their own traditions are those things that are offered in sacrifice to idols (1 Cor. 8:4,10/10:19,28 / Rev. 2:14/2:20). This is how they follow the example of Jezebel. Those that commit adultery with the New Testament Jezebel are those who have made vows to God that they will accept Jesus Christ as their example and their savior, but then afterward, they find comfort in embracing the false traditions that mankind has introduced to the Christian body of believers. Man's perverted influence on the servants of Jesus Christ is no different than that of the influence of Jezebel concerning how she introduced her native religion of Baal worship into the highest level of Israelite society.

The death bed and the great tribulation that God threatened to place the New Testament Jezebel and her followers in is the reprobate mind-state of a misinformed believer (Rom. 1:28-32). Although we may confess that we are children of God and that we accept Jesus Christ as our savior when we are misinformed concerning the will of God, how can we truly know if we love that which we have come to accept? If we pretend to believe in the righteousness of Jesus Christ, we will continually miss the mark and remain spiritually malnourished as we desire the peace that God has promised the body of Christ: the peace that passes all understanding: the peace that hypocrisy will never be able to provide us. We who are joined to the Jezebel(false church) of the New Testament must understand that God will reward us according to our deeds, which consist of us always learning but never receiving the ability to consistently manifest the true will of God (2 Tim. 3:1-7).

* * *

Neither the Jezebel of the Old Testament nor the Jezebel(false church) of the New Testament has anything to do with prostitution, sexual misconduct, or seduction in the physical sense. Jezebel of the Old Testament encouraged the children of Israel to go whoring after other gods and commit idolatry. God warned his people of this very thing, but they ignored the words that Moses had written and welcomed the false religion of Baal. Even so, at this present time, many of us acknowledge our belief in God, but we will not commit to God's righteousness. We will confess that we are one with God, but we will continually practice behavior that does not please God. We will also fellowship in the name of Jesus Christ while welcoming and accepting the abominable traditions introduced to the faith by those who place their own traditions above the example of Jesus Christ.

Although the Jezebel of the Old Testament was not a whore, she was a murderer. Although she was not a prostitute, she disregarded the law of the God of Israel. And although she was not an adulteress, she undeniably committed idolatry and influenced most of the children of Israel to do so. It was Baal that Jezebel believed in, and it was Baal that she accepted as her god. Jezebel was taught to worship Baal from her youth.

Jezebel was the daughter of a king and became the wife of a king. Jezebel loved her husband Ahab dearly and was dangerously supportive of him. When it comes to the relationship with her husband, unfaithful is not something that Jezebel could be called. She was very faithful to her husband and her god. Jezebel believed strongly in the traditional religion of her youth, and she sought to broadcast the religion of Baal wherever her influence could be felt. It is sad to say, but all of Jezebel's efforts to please her husband led to her death. For in the sight of the LORD, Jezebel's conduct was evil, wicked, and malicious. This is where Jezebel went wrong. But the insinuation that Jezebel was a whore, bears no evidence at all when the true story of Jezebel's life is opened for observation. The scriptures of the Bible, which show that Jezebel was not a whore have just been revealed in Divine Context.

Context #11 reveals how the words we accept that are spoken by the tongue can either lead us in the direction of death or life.

PROVERBS 18:21

21. Death and life *are* in the power of the tongue: and they that love it shall eat the fruit thereof.

Death And Life

Divine Context is understanding that when king Solomon said that "Death and life *are* in the power of the tongue," Solomon was not speaking in terms of us having the power or the ability to speak our fate into existence through the words that we speak out of our mouths.

* * *

From an infant child to a mature adult, so much of what we have learned in life has come from listening to others and accepting what others say, as opposed to us speaking to others. Many of our choices in life are the results of some type of verbal communication or the lack thereof. What we say to others can hurt them, but what we accept of others based on what they verbally express by the tongue can hurt us even more. This Divine Context was not written in order to bring attention to the things spoken by the tongue that can hurt our feelings. Rather, this Divine Context was written in order to bring attention to the words that are spoken by the tongue that we accept, which can damage our souls by leading us away from the acceptable the will of God.

When king Solomon spoke this proverb concerning death and life, he was not speaking in terms of the words that we speak concerning our daily lives apart from God's will. The death and life that Solomon is referring to are the righteous words of God, as opposed to the unrighteous words of man.

When we hear someone say that death and life are in the power of our tongue, we often begin to reflect on the notion that we somehow have the power to sway our lives in one direction or another by the things we speak. Within this Divine Context, we will try to eliminate these assumptions and concentrate on the true interpretation of the death and the life which Solomon is referring to. The truth of God's will is life, and every other word that mankind accepts other than God's word is death. The scripture speaks of death and life, but the scripture goes on to say, "**. . . and they that love it**(death or life) **shall eat the fruit thereof** [Pro. 18:21]."

As we accept the words of others, we are either going to consume the substance of life, or we are going to consume the substance of death. And as we move forward within this Divine Context, we must first accept that the truth of God's will is that which defines life. If we are obedient to God's will, then we are spiritually alive in the eyes of God. But if we are disobedient to God's will or ignore God's will, then we are spiritually dead in the eyes of God.

Unlike the New Testament, much of the Old Testament speaks of death in the literal sense. Within the New Testament, the consequences of being disobedient to God's will leave us spiritually separated from the peace that God's truth is able to give us (Rom. 2:5-11). But within the Old Testament, the consequences of being disobedient to God's will not only resulted in being spiritually separated from having a peaceful sense of right and wrong but also being disobedient to God's will usually resulted in a sentence of death literally.

A great example of the direction of death and life appears in the Old Testament book of Deuteronomy. As Moses declared the will of God to the children of Israel for the second time, Moses included these words saying, "**See, I have set before thee this day life and good, and death and evil; In that I command thee this day to love the LORD thy God, to walk in his ways, and to keep his commandments and his statutes and his judgments, that thou mayest live and multiply: and the LORD thy God shall bless thee in the land whither thou goest** to possess it. **But if thine heart turn away, so that thou wilt not hear, but shalt be drawn away, and worship other gods, and serve them; I denounce unto you this day, that ye shall surely perish**(die), ***and that* ye shall not prolong *your* days upon the land, whither thou passest over Jordan**(the Jordan river) **to go to possess it. I call heaven and earth to record this day against you,** *that* **I have set before you life and death, blessing and cursing: therefore choose life, that both thou and thy seed may live: That thou mayest love the LORD thy God,** *and* **that thou mayest obey his voice**(word), **and that thou mayest cleave unto him: for he** *is* **thy life, and the length of thy days: that thou mayest dwell in the land which the LORD sware unto thy fathers, to Abraham, to Isaac, and to Jacob, to give them** [Deu. 30:15-20]."

Within all that Moses declared to the children of Israel, Moses's definition of life was for the people to obey God's commandments, statutes, and judgments. On the other hand, Moses defined death in terms of the children of Israel turning their hearts away from God's established will, ignoring God's will, or being drawn away from God's will to serve other gods.

* * *

When the Bible speaks of life, it refers to the will of God. Obedience to the will of God is life. Moreover, there are examples in the Old Testament which reveal that there were those who, when they heard life being spoken, in their rebellion or in their ignorance, they chose to disregard the life that was being declared to them.

When God spoke to Moses concerning the children of Israel, saying, "**And I am come down to deliver them out of the hand of the Egyptians, and to bring them up out of that land unto a good land and a large, unto a land flowing with milk and honey . . .** [Exo. 3:8]." When the people of Israel heard this, they welcomed God's words with joy. Two years after delivering the children of Israel out of the land of Egypt, God was ready to give them the land of Canaan. Therefore, God commanded Moses to send out the men of war to search the land. Those same men became afraid of the inhabitants of the land, and when they returned, they spoke evil of the land that God had promised to give them, saying, "**The land, through which we have gone to search it, *is* a land that eateth up the inhabitants thereof; and all the people that we saw in it *are* men of a great stature** [Num. 13:32]." Choosing to ignore God's promise to fight for them, the men of war spoke death to the people of Israel.

Two men of the children of Israel by the name of Joshua and Caleb believed in God; therefore, they spoke life to the children of Israel by saying, "**The land, which we passed through to search it, *is* an exceeding good land. If the LORD delight in us, then he will bring us into this land, and give it us; a land which floweth with milk and honey. Only rebel not ye against the LORD, neither fear ye the people of the land; for they *are* bread for us: their defence is departed from them, and the LORD *is* with us: fear them not** [Num. 14:7-9]." Ironically the people threatened to stone Joshua and Caleb for speaking these words.

The words of death included an evil report that the men of war spoke to the people of Israel, telling them that they could not defeat the inhabitants of the land and that the land was not fit for them to live in. The words of encouragement that Joshua and Caleb offered to the people reminding them that obedience to God would ensure a victory, were the words of life.

The whole congregation chose to accept the evil report rather than accept God's will. The tongues of Joshua and Caleb spoke life, but the tongues of the men of war spoke death. The children of Israel did not have a believing heart; therefore, they chose death above the will of God. The whole congregation even began to complain, saying, "**Would**(We wish to) **God that we had died in the land of Egypt! or would**(we wish to) **God we had died in this wilderness! And wherefore hath the LORD brought us unto this land, to fall by the sword, that our wives and our children should be a prey? were it not better for us to return into Egypt? . . . Let us make a captain, and let us return into Egypt** [Num. 14:2-4]."

The people of Israel liked to consume the fruit of death; therefore, they chose to accept the words of the evil report from the men of war.

Death And Life

The consequences of their actions led to God deciding that the whole congregation would wander in the wilderness for thirty-eight more years until that entire adult generation of Israelites was dead. Joshua and Caleb were the only men of war that God allowed to remain alive and enter the land that he promised to give them. "Death and life *are* in the power of the tongue: and they that love it shall eat the fruit thereof [Pro. 18:21]."

* * *

When Jeroboam reigned as king over the kingdom of Israel in Samaria, God sent a man to the king in Bethel to curse the idolatrous altar that the king had made for the children of Israel to perform sacrifices on. Jeroboam was an evil king in the eyes of God. After the man of God had spoken to the king and cursed the altar, the king then said to the man of God, "**Come home with me, and refresh thyself, and I will give thee a reward** [1 Kings 13:7]." But the man of God replied to the king, saying, "**If thou wilt give me half thine house, I will not go in with thee, neither will I eat bread nor drink water in this place: For so was it charged me by the word of the LORD, saying, Eat no bread, nor drink water, nor turn again by the same way that thou camest** [1 Kings 13:8-9]."

The man of God obeyed God's word and went out from the king in a different way. Because he obeyed the word of God, it seemed as though the man of God had chosen life. But when an old prophet heard what the man of God had said and done to king Jeroboam, the old prophet went out and found the man of God sitting under an oak tree. The old prophet then said to the man of God, "**Come home with me, and eat bread** [1 Kings 13:15]." Once again, the man of God replied, saying, "**I may not return with thee, nor go in with thee: neither will I eat bread nor drink water with thee in this place: For it was said to me by the word of the LORD, Thou shalt eat no bread nor drink water there, nor turn again to go by the way that thou camest** [1 Kings 13:16-17]." The man of God continued to choose life.

Seeing that the man of God was determined to obey God's word, the old prophet then said to the man of God, "**I *am* a prophet also as** thou *art*; and an angel spake unto me by the word of the LORD, saying, Bring him back with thee into thine house, that he may eat bread and drink water [1 Kings 13:18]." Although it was a lie, the man of God believed the words of the old prophet and followed him to his house in Bethel.

As the old prophet and the man of God sat down at the table, the old prophet said to the man of God, "**Thus saith the LORD, Forasmuch as thou hast disobeyed the mouth(word) of the LORD, and hast not kept the commandment which the LORD thy God commanded thee, But camest back, and hast eaten bread and drunk water in the place, of the which *the Lord* did say to thee, Eat no bread, and drink no water; thy carcase shall not come unto the sepulcher(grave) of thy fathers** [1 Kings 13:21-22]." When all was said and done, the man of God had chosen death over life. And when he departed from the old prophet's house, the scripture says, "**And when he was gone, a lion met him by the way, and slew(killed) him: and his carcase(dead body) was cast in the way(road), and the ass(donkey) stood by it, the lion also stood by the carcase** [1 Kings 13:24]." For a while, the man of God held strong to the words that God had spoken to him, but then he became weak and believed the words of the old prophet. "Death and life *are* in the power of the tongue: and they that love it shall eat the fruit thereof [Pro. 18:31]."

* * *

During the ministry of the prophet Jeremiah, God sent Nebuchadnezzar, the king of Babylon to destroy Jerusalem and take the people of Judah into Babylon. The men that the king of Babylon left in charge of those who remained in the land were murdered by certain men of Israel. Then the poor people of the land became afraid of the king of Babylon. Therefore, rather than stay in Jerusalem, they desired to go down to Egypt, where they thought they would be safe. But before the people made up their minds, they asked Jeremiah to inquire of the LORD exactly what they should do. The people even said to Jeremiah, "**The LORD be a true and faithful witness between us, if we do not even** according to all things for the which the LORD thy God shall send thee to us. Whether *it be* good, or whether *it be* evil(unpleasant), we will obey the voice(word) of the LORD our God, to whom we send thee; that it may be well with us, when we obey the voice of the LORD our God [Jer. 42:5-6]."

Jeremiah asked the LORD what the people should do. When Jeremiah told them that the LORD said that they should not go to Egypt, but they should remain in the land and serve the king of Babylon, the leaders of the people responded to Jeremiah, saying, "**Thou speakest falsely: the LORD our God hath not sent thee to say, Go not into Egypt to sojourn there: But Baruch**(Jeremiah's friend) **the son of Neriah setteth thee on against us, for to deliver us into the hand of the Chaldeans**(Babylonians)**, that they might put us to death, and carry us away captives into Babylon** [Jer. 43:2-3]." The leaders of the people were willing to ignore the will of God and place their fate in their own hands.

The people listened to their leaders who rejected Jeremiah's words and went to Egypt, choosing death above life. Therefore, God said to Jeremiah that he would also send the king of Babylon to Egypt, and the king of Babylon would destroy Egypt and all those who went to Egypt (Jer. 43:8-13). Death was in the tongue of the leaders of the people, and life was in the tongue of the prophet Jeremiah. The people chose death and were destroyed along with all who dwelt in Egypt. "Death and life *are* in the power of the tongue: and they that love it shall eat the fruit thereof [Pro. 18: 21]."

* * *

We usually focus on the portion of the scripture that says, "Death and life *are* in the power of the tongue," but there is much more for us to consider. When we hear that Proverbs 18:21 says that the tongue has power, we do not wait to understand the full context of what the word "power" truly means. The word "power" within the scripture of Proverbs 18:21 refers to the direction of the tongue. The words of a person's tongue can either direct those who are listening towards that which is truth or towards that which is false. Whether it is the truth or whether it is falsehood that proceeds from the tongue, both have consequences. The consequences of truth are peace and justification in the sight of God, but the consequences of falsehood are ignorance and condemnation by God (Rom. 2:1-11).

We often focus on the portion of the scripture which says that the tongue has power because we like the idea of being able to speak things into existence. What we should be focusing on is the portion of scripture that says, "**. . . and they that love it**(death or life) **shall eat the fruit thereof** [Pro. 18:21]."

The previous examples of those who disobeyed God's will show that they chose to accept the fruit of falsehood that was presented to them. The problem was not that the men of war used their words to bring up an evil report about the land that God had promised to them. The problem was not the words that the old prophet used to speak to the man of God. And the problem was not the words of the leaders of the people who told Jeremiah that he was speaking falsely concerning the will of God.

For the people in the wilderness, the problem was that they chose to accept the words of the men of war above the will of God. For the man of God who cursed the altar in Bethel, the problem was that he chose to accept the words of the old prophet above the will of God. And for the people who were afraid of the king of Babylon and decided to go to Egypt, the problem was that they chose to accept the words of their leaders above the will of God.

Within each of these situations, we see that just as the words of death were present, so were the words of life. The word of God was the life that would lead the people in the right direction, but they chose to follow the words of death by rejecting the word of God. The consequences of rejecting life turned out to be deadly. "Death and life *are* in the power(direction) of the tongue: and they that love it shall eat the fruit thereof [Pro. 18:21]."

* * *

We cannot control what others say, but what we can control is how we accept what others say. As we begin to gain interest in the will of God, we must be very careful of the words that we accept from others. And, how we accept those words from others is very important also. Yes, we should cherish the relationships that we share with each other as members of the body of Christ. Nevertheless, as we communicate with one another, we must also search the scriptures for context so that we can confirm or reject what we are hearing. Even Jesus Christ warned his disciples of this very same thing.

The words of Jesus Christ are very important because he is the chief messenger of God's new covenant. While Jesus Christ went through the cities and the villages of Judaea, there were gathered to him many people seeking to hear him speak. Jesus began by speaking a parable about a Sower who went and sowed seeds. As the parable goes, some of the seeds fell by the wayside, some seeds fell on stony places, some seeds fell among thorns, and some seeds fell into good ground (Mat. 13:3-9). The Sower is Jesus Christ, and the seeds are the words of God (Luke 8:11-15). Once Jesus explained to his disciples the true interpretation of this parable, Jesus then said, "**Take heed therefore how ye hear: for whosoever hath** (understanding)**, to him shall be given**(understanding)**; and whosoever hath not** (understanding)**, from him shall be taken even that**(the understanding) **which he seemeth to have** [Luke 8:18]."

The authors of the New Testament spoke about the direction of the tongue more than anything else. In almost every letter that is written within the New Testament, the authors always warned the believers about those who would come along and pervert the gospel of Jesus Christ in order to lead the disciples astray.

The Apostle Paul was the leading apostle of his generation. Paul wrote over half of the letters within the New Testament. At the end of Paul's last missionary journey, he warned the elders of the city of Ephesus, saying, "**Wherefore I take you to record this day, that I *am* pure from the blood of all *men*. For I have not shunned to declare unto you all the counsel of God. Take heed therefore unto yourselves, and to all the flock**(believers)**, over the which the Holy Ghost hath** made you overseers(leaders), **to feed the church of God, which he hath purchased with his own blood. For I know this, that after my departing**(death) **shall grievous wolves enter in among you, not sparing the flock. Also of your own selves shall men arise, speaking perverse**(false) **things, to draw away disciples after them** [Acts 20:26-30]." Paul constantly warned the disciples in almost every letter to be aware of those who would alter the truth of the gospel through their words (2 Pet. 3:15-16).

James was a disciple of Jesus Christ, and he was also an author of the New Testament. Within his letter to the believers, James did not pull any punches when he wrote of the dangers of the tongue. The subject matter of the letter of James is wisdom. When speaking of the dangers of the tongue, James says, "**And the tongue *is* a fire, a world of iniquity: so is the tongue among our members, that it defileth the whole body, and setteth on fire the course of nature; and it is set on fire of hell. For every kind of beasts, and of birds, and of serpents, and of things in the sea, is tamed, and hath been tamed of mankind: But the tongue can no man tame; *it is* an unruly evil, full of deadly poison** [Jam. 3:6-8]." If we are not careful to search the scriptures for context as we listen to others preach the gospel of Christ, we can sometimes accept death when we assume that we are accepting life. "Death and life *are* in the power(direction) of the tongue: and they that love it shall eat the fruit thereof [Pro. 18:21]."

Moreover, the Apostle Peter was also an author of the New Testament, and he also spoke of those who would treat the disciples of Christ like their own property, influencing them to follow their traditions by speaking perverted words (2 Pet. 1:21-2:1-3). Peter was present with the Lord Jesus Christ; therefore, Peter's advice to the believers carried much weight. Peter understood that there would be danger even after we begin to believe in Jesus Christ. The direction of the words of the tongue dominates Peter's second letter. When speaking of those who use their tongues to speak death, Peter describes how they trap others, saying, "**For when they speak great swelling *words* of vanity, they allure through the lusts of the flesh, *through much* wantonness**(excess)**, those that were clean escaped from**

them who live in error [2 Pet. 2:18]." The letter of 2 Peter allows us to understand that even when we overcome the world through the knowledge of the Lord Jesus Christ, there remains danger from within by many of those who falsely claim to belong to Christ. "Death and life *are* in the power(direction) of the tongue: and they that love it shall eat the fruit thereof [Pro. 18:21]."

* * *

We are taught to speak it and claim it. We are taught to be careful what we say because it will come to pass. We are taught to speak it and believe that it will be ours. All these assumptions are inspired by the idea that somehow power dwells within our tongues, and what we say can predict the outcome of our tomorrow. To a certain degree, we must admit that this is true because the words that we speak are usually inspired by the thoughts within our minds and the intentions of our hearts. The words of our tongue often confirm what we are thinking or what we have already thought. Therefore, the situations that we find ourselves in are based more on our thought process rather than the words that we speak using our tongues.

The words of our tongue can get us into trouble when our words offend the established principles, and the words of our tongue can get us out of trouble when we use our words to confirm and justify the established principles. The words of our tongue can please God, but they can also displease God. The words of our tongue can represent God's will, and the words of our tongue can also misrepresent God's will. The greatest communication source ever given to mankind is the tongue. The direction of the tongue can build empires, and the direction of the tongue can also destroy worlds. The direction of the tongue can solidify a loving relationship, and the direction of the tongue can also destroy that selfsame relationship in an instant. Our tongues and the direction of the words which proceed from our tongues can surely have a profound effect on the lives of others.

Those who would much rather follow their own will are more susceptible to consuming the fruit of death from those who flatter them through words that they want to hear rather than through words that truly represent God's will. But we who would much rather choose God's will above our own personal will are those who first search the scriptures for context and then consume the fruit of life from those who sincerely speak the truth of the gospel.

The book of Proverbs is said to be a book of dark sayings that are obscure, as in mysterious (Pro. 1:1-6). The subject matter contained within the book of Proverbs is knowledge, understanding, and wisdom. As babes in Christ, we may know something, although we do not understand exactly what we know. As young men and women in Christ, we may understand something, although we are not wise enough to endure in the manifest example of those things that we understand. Wisdom is the ultimate goal in all that we put our hearts and minds to do. Wisdom is not measured in how much we know. Neither is wisdom measured in how much we understand. Wisdom, according to God's will, is measured by reverence and obedience: reverence that shows respect for God because he is God and obedience that separates death and life and is justified by God.

Please understand that the power of the tongue spoken of in Proverbs 18:21 is not referring to the ability to literally speak death or life upon ourselves. According to Proverbs 18:21, the death(unrighteousness) and the life(righteousness) that we bring on ourselves usually come as the result of our behavior due to what we have heard and accepted from others. Also, according to Proverbs 18:21, the power of the tongue is not referring to verbally claiming things that we desire or believing that the words of our tongue will somehow make it all come to pass. The accomplishments that God allows us to achieve in life are orchestrated by our opportunities and through our efforts, regardless of whether we use our tongues to speak one word towards our future or not. The scripture of Proverbs 18:21 was written concerning those who speak either truth or falsehood concerning God's will through the words that proceed from the tongue and those who choose to accept either true or false concerning God's will through the words that proceed from the tongue.

The most important information that we need to know when

listening to those who declare the word of God is not what we hear but rather how we accept what we hear. Because unrighteousness and righteousness are in the direction of the words of the tongue, and those who love either unrighteousness or righteousness shall consume the substance thereof. Please, my fellow brothers and sisters in Christ, pray that we choose wisely! Death and life have just been revealed in Divine Context.

Context #12 reveals how God made peace for the children of Israel after he created all the evil that came upon them.

ISAIAH 45:5-7

5. I *am* the LORD, and *there is* none else, *there is* no God beside me: I girded thee, though thou hast not known me:

6. That they may know from the rising of the sun, and from the west, that *there is* none beside me. I *am* the LORD, and *there is* none else.

7. I form the light, and create darkness: I make peace, and create evil: I the LORD do all these *things*.

I Make Peace And Create Evil

Divine Context is understanding that the peace that God made was the Persian king Cyrus releasing the children of Israel from captivity after seventy years, and the evil that God created was the invasion of Jerusalem by the Babylonian king Nebuchadnezzar, which led to their seventy years of captivity.

* * *

God is good all the time, and all the time God is good. If this is so, how can the prophet Isaiah say that God creates evil? I know that my God is not evil. But how can this be? How is the right question because the true context of the scriptures will reveal exactly how God made peace after creating evil.

The word "evil" spoken by the prophet Isaiah is in the manner of God allowing distress, affliction, and sorrow to come on the children of Israel. The evil that Isaiah spoke of does not, however, refer to blatant maliciousness manifested by God, insinuating that God was looking forward to bringing harm to the Israelites for no reason at all. God is a God of judgment, and the evil that God caused to come on the Israelites was their destruction and captivity by the Babylonian king Nebuchadnezzar.

Before we get into the evil that God created, let us first take a good look at the peace that God had already pronounced long before destruction and misery came to the children of Israel. God allowed all this evil to come on the Israelites so that his people could know that their God was a God of judgment, a God of mercy, and the only living God.

For us to read a scripture claiming that God creates evil gives us second thoughts about God being all-loving. Within the New Testament, God is spoken of as a God of grace and mercy, not a God of darkness and evil. The New Testament standard that Jesus Christ introduced to the world brought grace with it: this grace is far removed from the standard of judgment contained within the Old Testament.

Although the standards may have changed, the God of the Old Testament era is, in many ways, the same God of the New Testament. Take a look at our current global situation. It is easy for us to recognize many inhumane events and see the distress, the sorrow, and the affliction that inhabits almost every corner of the planet. The God of the Old Testament is the same God of the New Testament, although God is now judging those who believe in Jesus Christ by the faith of Christ rather than by the works of the Old Testament law of Moses.

Isaiah 45:7 is only one scripture out of a thousand or so scriptures contained within the entire book of Isaiah. When reading the words of the Bible, at times, we can become mesmerized by certain verses or chapters, not realizing that the words of each book are to be read as a personal invitation into the manifold wisdom of God. Each book, letter, and psalm is meant to be read in its entirety and comprehended not by just one scripture or one chapter but by all that is written and declared therein.

For what purpose did God pronounce that it is he who makes peace and that it is he who creates evil? Human beings should clearly understand the selfishness of wanting to be recognized for all that we accomplish. We do not become overjoyed when someone else gets all the credit and all the glory for something that we have made or created ourselves. God also seeks to receive the credit and the recognition for all his works and accomplishments. God promised to build the children of Israel into a holy nation (Exo. 19:5-6). For hundreds of years, God was patient with his chosen people as they went through their growing pains. Eventually, the Israelites became the strong nation that was long ago promised to their forefathers by God (2 Sam. 7:22-24).

For many decades, God allowed his people to experience years of prosperity and years of distress and sorrow, but God always kept them in the place where he planted them: Jerusalem (2 Chr. 6:1-6). Amid all the blessings that came to the Israelites, they always found a way to give sculptured stones or some form of a pagan god the credit that belonged to the true and living God. In all their afflictions, God would ease his anger and make a way for his people to remain in the land which he promised. God gave them the land of Canaan, and it was theirs. God did all that he could to uphold his part of the covenant with the Israelites. Being the God that he is, several verses before he proclaimed the destruction of his people in Isaiah 45:7, God also gave his people hope as a sign that he still loved them, saying, "... **I have formed thee; thou *art* my servant: O Israel, thou shalt not be forgotten of me** [Isa. 44:21]."

Evil was on its way, but God would not forget about his chosen people. Everyone knows that during times of joy and prosperity, God gets all the thanks. But during times of despair, in some form or fashion, we all feel that God has forgotten about us. God is not ignorant of this fact. For this reason, God wanted the children of Israel to acknowledge that it was he who created the distress that they would experience. God also wanted his people to acknowledge the favor that they would experience because of him. Isaiah continued to present the word of the LORD to the Israelites, saying, "**I (the LORD) have blotted out, as a thick cloud, thy transgressions, and, as a cloud, thy sins: return unto me; for I have redeemed thee. Sing, O ye heavens; for the LORD hath done *it*: shout, ye lower parts of the earth: break forth into singing, ye mountains, O forest, and every tree therein: for the LORD hath redeemed Jacob, and glorified himself in Israel** [Isa. 44:22-23]." God was telling the children of Israel beforehand that he would, in due time, blot out their transgressions and their sins. God said these things in reference to his people's release from captivity: not their release from the former captivity in Egypt, but rather their relief from the captivity that had not yet arrived but was sure to come.

If we were present during the era of Isaiah's ministry, we would have thought that Isaiah was insane or simply babbling, just like many of the people of Isaiah's generation. At this present time in history, we are truly blessed to have the volume of God's word composed within the Bible. We have easy access to a portion of mankind's history through the recorded history of the children of Israel. If we were present with Isaiah over twenty-five hundred years ago when he first spoke these words, we would not have a clue what Isaiah was saying about God making peace and creating evil.

The kingdom of Judah (the southern kingdom of Israel) and the inhabitants of the city of Jerusalem is who Isaiah is speaking to (2 Kings 19:1-2 / 2 Chr. 26:22). Speaking in the past tense, Isaiah said that God had blotted out the children of Israel's sins. Isaiah also said that God had redeemed the children of Israel. Redeemed the children of Israel from what? Blotted out their transgressions and their sins, when?

A few generations after Isaiah spoke these words, the kingdom of Judah and their capital city Jerusalem was destroyed by Nebuchadnezzar, the king of Babylon (2 Kings 24-25). Before Nebuchadnezzar came and destroyed the city of Jerusalem, God had already put an exit plan in place for his people. Over fifty years before Nebuchadnezzar took the children of Israel into captivity, Isaiah spoke to the people of Israel, saying, "**Thus saith the LORD, thy redeemer, and he that formed thee**(Israel) **from the womb, I** *am* **the LORD that maketh all** *things*; **that stretcheth forth the heavens alone; that spreadeth abroad the earth by myself; That frustrateth the tokens**(words) **of the liars, and maketh diviners**(those who guess) **mad**(foolish); **that turneth wise** *men* **backward, and maketh their knowledge foolish; That confirmeth the word of his servant** (Isaiah), **and performeth the counsel of his messengers; that saith to Jerusalem, Thou shalt be inhabited; and to the cities of Judah, Ye shall be built, and I will raise up the decayed places thereof: That saith to the deep, Be dry, and I will dry up thy rivers: That saith of Cyrus,** *He is* **my shepherd, and shall perform all my pleasure: even saying to Jerusalem, Thou**

shalt be built; and to the temple, Thy foundation shall be laid [Isa. 44:24-28]."

Cyrus? Your shepherd who shall perform all your pleasure? Who is this Cyrus that the prophet Isaiah is speaking of? Cyrus was the king of the Persian Empire who would eventually reign over Babylon and release the people of Israel from captivity, allowing them to return to Jerusalem and rebuild the temple of the LORD that king Solomon built. This is not something that Isaiah's generation would have figured out. Cyrus was not the king of Persia when Isaiah spoke these words. In fact, Cyrus was not even born at this time. The thoughts of that present generation would have been that Cyrus was an Israelite king who was to come. Someone named Cyrus of another nation would not have crossed their minds, especially not someone of another nation named Cyrus who would allow the rebuilding of the city of Jerusalem along with the temple of the LORD.

The nation of Israel, the kingdom of Judah to be exact, became the poster child for wickedness. They were God's people. They held the sacred oracles of the living God. They were proud in heart to confess that they belonged to the God that created heaven and earth. But their actions revealed that they did not care about God. God had become something to acknowledge rather than the one to obey. God had given the children of Israel the law of Moses as the standard-bearer for their laws and their judgments. As the years passed, the law of Moses literally became a none factor in the lives of the Israelites. Zedekiah was the king of Judah when the Babylonians destroyed Jerusalem and took the people captive. It was Zedekiah's father, Josiah, who tried his best to restore the daily rituals and customs of Moses back into the lives of the children of Israel.

An unnamed prophet of God spoke thirteen generations before Josiah's birth, saying that it would be a king by the name of Josiah who would reap vengeance on the unholy priests that Jeroboam, the former king of Israel, had appointed. When Josiah began to reign over Judah, he did just that.

At the age of twenty-six, Josiah began to clean up the mess that the former kings of Judah had made. Josiah began to repair the house of the

LORD and dismantle all the high places where the Israelites worshiped idols. In the process of repairing the temple, the high priest found the book of the law of Moses in the house of the LORD. The book of the law of Moses was then brought before king Josiah, and they read it to him. When Josiah heard the words of the book, he became grieved because of the things that were being read to him (2 Kings 22:1-11). Then Josiah spoke to his servants, saying, "**Go ye, enquire of the LORD for me, and for the people, and for all Judah, concerning the words of this book that is found: for great** *is* **the wrath of the LORD that is kindled against us, because our fathers have not hearkened**(listened) **unto the words of this book, to do according unto all that which is written concerning us** [2 Kings 22:13]."

The high priest spoke to the prophetess Huldah, and she inquired of the LORD on behalf of king Josiah. The prophetess then said to the high priest, "**Thus saith the LORD God of Israel, Tell the man that sent you to me, Thus saith the LORD, Behold, I bring evil upon this place, and upon the inhabitants thereof,** *even* **all the words of the book which the king of Judah hath read: Because they have forsaken me, and have burned incense unto other gods, that they might provoke me to anger with all the works of their hands; therefore my wrath shall be kindled against this place, and shall not be quenched. But to the king of Judah which sent you to enquire of the LORD, thus shall ye say to him, Thus saith the LORD God of Israel,** *As touching* **the words which thou hast heard: Because thine heart was tender, and thou hast humbled thyself before the LORD, when thou heardest what I spake against this place, and against the inhabitants thereof, that they should become a desolation and a curse, and hast rent**(torn) **thy clothes, and wept before me; I also have heard** *thee*, **saith the LORD. Behold therefore, I will gather thee unto thy fathers, and thou shalt be gathered into thy grave in peace; and thine eyes shall not see all the evil which I will bring upon this place** [2 Kings 22:15-20]." Who was going to bring evil on Jerusalem? It was God who would bring evil on the kingdom of Israel because of their transgressions.

God recognized the efforts of Josiah and did not allow the evil to happen to Jerusalem while he was king. But the evil that would eventually come on the land of Judah was no secret. For even the prophet Jeremiah was bold in his declarations of the Israelite's pending sorrows.

A few generations after the prophet Isaiah spoke of the evil that would come to the land of Judah, Jeremiah also spoke to the people of Judah, saying, "**Therefore thus saith the LORD of hosts; Because ye have not heard my words, Behold, I will send and take all the families**(Gentiles) **of the north, saith the LORD, and Nebuchadrezzar the king of Babylon, my servant, and will bring them against this land, and against the inhabitants thereof, and against all these nations round about, and will utterly destroy them, and make them an astonishment, and an hissing, and perpetual desolations. Moreover I will take from them the voice of mirth, and the voice of gladness, the voice of the bridegroom, and the voice of the bride, the sound of the millstones, and the light of the candle. And this whole land shall be a desolation,** *and* **an astonishment; and these nations shall serve the king of Babylon seventy years** [Jer. 25:8-11]."

The LORD said that the destruction caused by the king of Babylon will be the cup that every nation shall drink of. Those nations that were not even subject to the law of Moses would reap the vengeance of God. Those other nations felt compelled to dismiss the words of Jeremiah. This was when God's feelings got involved. As Jeremiah spoke to all the other nations about how God would bring evil to his own people, he assured them that God would bring evil on all the other nations also (Jer. 25:29).

Although Jeremiah told all the other nations that they would become subject to the Babylonians, Jeremiah wrote a letter to the children of Israel concerning their fate, in which he said, "**For thus saith the LORD, That after seventy years be accomplished at Babylon I will visit you, and perform my good word toward you, in causing you to return to this place**(Jerusalem) [Jer. 29:10]." The words of Jeremiah's letter said nothing about exactly how God would bring about their return to Jerusalem, only that they would return.

While Josiah's son Zedekiah was king over the land of Judah, Nebuchadnezzar the king of Babylon, captured the city of Jerusalem and burnt down the house of the LORD along with the wall that surrounded Jerusalem. Nebuchadnezzar then took most of the people back to Babylon as his captives, and he killed all the mighty men of Judah, including king Zedekiah's sons. He then put out Zedekiah's eyes, blinding him so that he could never again see the land that he once ruled.

Not all the people of Judah were carried away to Babylon. Nebuchadnezzar let those who were poor remain in the country and gave them vineyards and fields, but he carried the king of Judah to Babylon. It was evident that the evil that God created had finally manifested itself in the land of the Israelites.

* * *

For seventy years, the children of Israel remained captives in Babylon. These are the years of the prophet Daniel. Daniel was a child when he was taken into captivity, and he was fortunate enough to see the release of his people seventy years later (2 Kings 24:1-5 / Dan. 1:1-4). Once the Median and the Persian empire began to reign over the Babylonians, the governors of the Median kingdom devised a plot to have Daniel eaten by lions. Rather than allow Daniel to be eaten by lions, God found Daniel to be innocent in his cause, and the lions refused to harm him. Darius, the king of the Median and the Persian empire, loved Daniel and was relieved to see that God had saved him. Daniel's experience jump-started the process of the peace that God had promised to the children of Israel through the prophets Isaiah and Jeremiah.

Once king Darius saw that God delivered Daniel from the mouth of the lions, Darius told all the people of the earth that they should tremble and fear before the God of Daniel (Dan. 6:25-27). Then the scripture goes on to say, "**So this Daniel prospered in the reign of Darius, and in the reign of Cyrus the Persian** [Dan. 6:28]." Cyrus the Persian is who the prophet Isaiah said would bring peace to the people of Israel at least fifty years before the prophet Jeremiah spoke of all the evil that king Nebuchadnezzar would work among the children of Israel in Jerusalem. Once Isaiah spoke of the peace that Cyrus would bring, it was over one hundred and twenty years later that Cyrus would come and bring peace to the thoughts of the children of Israel.

Before the prophet Jeremiah was born, even before Jeremiah's parents were born, the prophet Isaiah said that Cyrus would perform all of God's pleasure concerning the children of Israel. Isaiah mentioned that king Cyrus would be the person who would say to the city of Jerusalem, "... **Thou shalt be built**... [Isa. 44:28]," and to the temple of the LORD that was in Jerusalem, "... **Thy foundation shall be laid** [Isa. 44:28]."

Over two hundred years before king Cyrus would reign over Babylon, God spoke of how Cyrus was his shepherd. The writings of Isaiah certainly had an impact on king Cyrus' decision to release the children of Israel and allow them to return to their homeland. Cyrus did not let the Jews return to Jerusalem after seventy years of captivity to go and do whatever their hearts desired. The children of Israel could not call themselves an independent nation because although they were allowed to return to their homeland of Judah, they were still subject to the laws and the governing of the Median and the Persian empire.

Cyrus was truly merciful to the Jews. Respecting the words of Isaiah, the former prophet of the children of Israel, Cyrus granted the Jews their release. Within the proclamation that Cyrus sent throughout his kingdom, he let it be known why the Jews were on their way back home.

In his first year on the throne, Cyrus put his words in writing, saying, "**Thus saith Cyrus king of Persia, The LORD God of heaven hath given me all the kingdoms of the earth; and he hath charged me to build him an house at Jerusalem, which *is* in Judah. Who *is there* among you of all his people? his God be with him, and let him go up to Jerusalem, which *is* in Judah, and build the house of the LORD God of Israel, (he *is* the God,) which *is* in Jerusalem. And whosoever remaineth in any place where he sojourneth, let the men of his place help him with silver, and with gold, and with goods, and with beasts, beside the freewill offering for the house of God that *is* in Jerusalem** [Ezra 1:2-4]." The peace that God promised to make for the children of Israel was finally showing itself. Now the very same Cyrus that Isaiah spoke of was known to the children of Israel. Now the children of Israel could lay their eyes on Cyrus. Now the children of Israel could believe with their whole hearts that there is no other living god besides the God of Israel. This is exactly what God wanted the children of Israel to realize. The God of Israel was God, and he was the only God that held their fate in his hand.

* * *

There was a time in my life when I was locked away in prison for committing crimes against the government of the United States. It was a painful time for many of my close friends and family members also. They prayed to God for my release daily and looked for hope in almost anything that sounded remotely familiar to my situation. While in prison, I turned to God and began to learn about the Bible and Jesus Christ. It came to pass that one of my siblings wrote to me, and within her letter, she included Isaiah 45:1-4, which says, "**THUS saith the LORD to his anointed, to Cyrus, whose right hand I have holden**(strengthened), **to subdue nations before him; and I will loose the loins of kings, to open before him the two leaved gates; and the gates shall not be shut; I will go before thee, and make the crooked places straight: I will break in pieces the gates of brass, and cut in sunder the bars of iron: And I will give thee the treasures of darkness, and hidden riches of secret places, that thou mayest know that I, the LORD, which call *thee* by thy name, *am* the God of Israel. For Jacob my servant's sake, and Israel mine elect, I have even called thee**(Cyrus) **by thy name: I have surnamed thee, though thou hast not known me.**" The fact that the scriptures mentioned something about opening gates that would not be shut, my sister sent these few scriptures to me so that I could somehow believe that these specific words of the prophet Isaiah were related to my present situation.

As I began to read these verses within the book of Isaiah, I became somewhat sad. I was sad because although my sister's intentions were sincere, her understanding of the scriptures was misdirected. No scripture of the Bible's historical events should be equated to a situation that is taking place in our present lives. If we choose to use historical Biblical events to inspire encouragement concerning our current situations, we must do so in the proper manner. This manner includes first explaining the true context of the historical event in its entirety and then relating the event to the present situation at hand. But if the true and detailed interpretation of the historical event is not established first, there will be no way to comprehend if the present situation should or should not be compared to the historical event that is documented within God's sacred word. This will leave us ignorant and perverted in our application of the scriptures into our lives and render our thoughts concerning the will of God distorted.

* * *

I am amazed at how small the Bible becomes when we begin to understand what we are reading and how we are to apply what we are reading into our everyday lives. Within the first few verses of the book of Ezra, king Cyrus says that God had given him all the kingdoms of the earth and charged him to build a house in Jerusalem. If we are not familiar with the words of the prophet Isaiah, we could think that God spoke directly to king Cyrus or appeared to Cyrus in some sort of vision, revealing these things to Cyrus. But that was not the case. Cyrus was saying that God had given all the nations of the earth into his power because of the prophecies of Isaiah that were shown to him by the children of Israel: and Cyrus believed the word of God. So, Cyrus acted on the prophesies that Isaiah wrote concerning him, feeling that his position as the king of Persia was truly ordained by the LORD God of heaven, the God of Israel.

The words of Ezra and Nehemiah were spoken over a hundred years after the words of the prophet Isaiah; nevertheless, the words that are written within the book of Ezra and Nehemiah are a confirmation of the words of the prophet Isaiah. And once we understand this, the subject matter of the book of Ezra and the subject matter of the book of Nehemiah becomes magnified because the prophet Isaiah is speaking beforehand concerning the events that would eventually take place within the books of Ezra and Nehemiah.

Receiving the true context of the word of God is one of the most important aspects of building our relationship with God through his word. To be honest, there is no other way to build a relationship with God but through his word. As we read Isaiah 44:28, which says, "**. . . Cyrus, *He is* my shepherd, and shall perform all my pleasure; even saying to Jerusalem, Thou shalt be built; and to the temple, Thy foundation shall be laid**," we are also reading the Old Testament books of Ezra and Nehemiah. It was their generation that rebuilt the temple of the LORD after seventy years of captivity. And it was during their time in history that the city of Jerusalem was first rebuilt. It was this king Cyrus that God opened the gates for. It was this king Cyrus that God spoke of, saying, "**I *am* the LORD, and *there is* none else, *there* is no God beside me: I girded**(prepared) **thee**(Cyrus)**, though thou**(Cyrus) **hast not known me: That they may know from the rising of the sun**(east)**, and from the west, that *there is* none beside me. I *am* the LORD, and *there is* none else. I form the light, and create darkness: I make peace, and create evil: I the LORD do all these *things*** [Isa. 45:5-7]."

The evil that God created was the misery, the destruction, and the affliction that Nebuchadnezzar, the king of Babylon, brought to the kingdom of Judah and their capital city Jerusalem. This evil was created because of the promises that God made to their forefathers long ago through Moses, saying, "**If thou wilt not observe to do all the words of this law** (the law of Moses) **that are written in this book, that thou mayest fear this glorious and fearful name, THE LORD THY GOD; Then the LORD will make thy plagues wonderful, and the plagues of thy seed, *even* great plagues, and of long continuance, and sore sicknesses, and of long continuance.**" "**And ye shall be left few in number, whereas ye were as the stars of heaven for multitude; because thou wouldest not obey the voice of the LORD thy God. And it shall come to pass, *that* as the LORD rejoiced over you to do you good, and to multiply you; so the LORD will rejoice over you to destroy you, and to bring you to nought**(nothing)**; and ye shall be plucked from off the land whither**(where) **thou goest to possess it** [Deu. 28:58-59,62-63]." It was through the Babylonian king

Nebuchadnezzar that approximately a thousand years after Moses spoke these words to the children of Israel, these promises came to pass.

Indeed, the LORD created evil and darkness by allowing king Nebuchadnezzar to take the children of Israel into captivity for seventy years. And indeed, the LORD made peace and light when he also allowed king Cyrus to let the children of Israel return to Jerusalem after seventy years. But the main purpose of all this evil, and the main purpose of all this peace, was so that the children of Israel, along with the world, might know that the God of Israel was the one and only living God. There is no other god beside him. There was no other god before him. There will not be another god that should follow him.

The main purpose of the birth, the childhood, and the reign of king Cyrus was to reveal to the world through the sacred writings of the prophet Isaiah that the God of Israel was the only living God. Therefore before Isaiah mentioned the name of king Cyrus, he said to the people of Israel, "**Thus saith the LORD, thy**(Israel's) **redeemer, and he that formed thee**(the nation of Israel) **from the womb, I *am* the LORD that maketh all *things*; that stretcheth forth the heavens alone; that spreadeth abroad the earth by myself; That frustrateth the tokens**(words) **of the liars, and maketh diviners**(those who guess) **mad**(foolish)**; that turneth wise *men* backward, and maketh their knowledge foolish; That confirmeth the word of his servant** (Isaiah), **and performeth the counsel of his messengers; that saith to Jerusalem, Thou shalt be inhabited, and to the cities of Judah, Ye shall be built . . .** [Isa. 44:24-26]."

Before God said that it is he that makes peace and that it is he that creates evil, God said to king Cyrus, "**. . . I girded**(prepared) **thee**(Cyrus)**, though thou**(Cyrus) **hast not known me . . .** [Isa. 45:5]." Within each of our lives, the power of God exists. Just as king Cyrus and king Nebuchadnezzar held their purpose within God's will, even so, are we subject to God's continual plan for the events that occur here on earth. I humbly pray to our Father that his plans for us include making peace rather than creating evil. We believe in a God of judgment, and we also believe in a God of mercy. Therefore, we also must recognize that the afflictions and the distress that we may be enduring today can soon result in the peace that we sincerely bask in tomorrow.

All these things are written so that we can believe and understand that there is one God and that there is no other god besides the living God. The Babylonians may have brought darkness and evil to the doorsteps of the children of Israel, but seventy years later, as an unstoppable force, the Persian king Cyrus brought light and peace back into the lives of the children of Israel. Our everyday struggles in life are not in vain. As we enjoy our times of favor and peace, thanking God for it all, let us remember to also be thankful as we struggle with our afflictions. How God made peace and how God created evil has just been revealed in Divine Context.

Context #13 reveals that the weapons that God will not allow to prosper are those weapons that directly oppose the righteousness of Jesus Christ that has been placed within the hearts and minds of Christ's disciples.

ISAIAH 54:15-17

15. Behold, they shall surely gather together, *but* not by me: whosoever shall gather together against thee shall fall for thy sake.

16. Behold, I have created the smith that bloweth the coals in the fire, and that bringeth forth an instrument for his work; and I have created the waster to destroy.

17. No weapon that is formed against thee shall prosper; and every tongue *that* shall rise against thee in judgment thou shalt condemn. This *is* the heritage of the servants of the LORD, and their righteousness *is* of me, saith the LORD.

No Weapon Formed Against Thee Shall Prosper

Divine Context is understanding that the weapons that shall not prosper against us are not the obstacles of our everyday lives that hinder us from satisfying our own self-serving desires. On the contrary, the weapons of Isaiah 54:17 are all the words, all the teachings, and all the traditional religious systems that contradict the righteousness of our Lord Jesus Christ.

* * *

The saying "No weapon that is formed against thee shall prosper" has been directed towards the actions of people who do certain things to hold us back from achieving many of our self-serving goals of gaining an advantage in particular situations. Go to any church or attend any Christian fellowship and bring up the scripture of Isaiah 54:17. Before anyone identifies Isaiah's words as referring to the weapons of false doctrines, they will often direct the words "no weapon that is formed against thee shall prosper" towards someone or something holding them back from a desired carnal goal. How do I know this? Because I have been there myself, and I have witnessed many others, along with myself, traveling down the same path of ignorance.

Receiving the words "no weapon that is formed against thee shall prosper" out of context almost cost me my life. Before I was given the Holy Ghost through the grace of God, I was truly a servant of myself. As a young child, my family structure was very stable. But before I became a teenager, my father passed away suddenly without warning, and life's direction for me became scattered all over the place. My mother tried her best to keep up with me, but having to work multiple jobs to support me and my two older brothers, she could not keep up with the mischievous mind of a young boy.

It was not long after I graduated from high school that I began selling drugs. My life of crime held many faces. I was into a little bit of everything, but when it came to dealing drugs, I really got into that. I experienced many years of arrests for all sorts of crimes, and I always came out squeaky clean. As I continued to wiggle out from under the law, I began to develop a false sense of security. Although I was yet to figure out who or what God was, I felt as if God was protecting me from all those who tried to bring me down. In my mind, whatever or whoever God was, he was on my side.

Shortly after I turned twenty-seven years old, I was indicted on federal drug conspiracy charges. My case is what you would call a dry conspiracy. The only evidence that the government provided against me were statements of several individuals who said that they either purchased drugs from me, saw me with drugs, or heard me talking about drugs. The government's evidence did not consist of physical drugs or physical money. There were no assets or property seized from me. The government did not produce telephone conversations, photos, audio recordings, or an electronic paper trail. Nevertheless, I was still indicted by a grand jury on drug conspiracy charges.

At the time of my indictment, I was not a religious person at all, but I did believe there was a God. A few years prior to my arrest, I tried my best to read the Bible. I considered myself to be more spiritual rather than religious. I had a feeling that all things happen for a reason and that God was real.

My arrest was a relief to me in many ways. Now I had a great reason to stop selling drugs. With so many individuals depending on me before my arrest, I felt that I had to constantly sell drugs to keep everyone happy. Although my life seemed to be prosperous on the outside, on the inside, my heart and my soul were lost because I knew that I was not experiencing what life was truly all about.

Less than six months after I was arrested, I gave my life to Christ, and I asked God to allow the ways of Jesus to lead me. For my whole life, I have been a fighter. I was not good at losing. The government's case produced many individuals who told the truth concerning my crimes. However, their case against me also produced many individuals who either told half the truth or outright lies about their association with me. I did not want to go to prison. I wanted to go home. If I were to tell the truth, and admit that I was guilty of the charges against me, I would have to serve a long prison sentence. If I decided to fight all the charges and go to trial, I could go scot-free. Then again, if I was found guilty at trial, I would have to serve a life sentence in prison.

Being deceived by my own selfish desires to go free, I decided to fight the charges by concentrating on all the lies that the government's witnesses spoke concerning me. I used my time in the county jail to read the Bible and become more familiar with God's will. The more I read the Bible, the more it seemed as if every situation in the Bible that delt with prison, bondage, false witnesses, and oppression fit my own personal situation. In time, I learned that the only reason why many situations in the Bible fit my own personal situation is that, in my ignorance, I forced them to. I began to deceive myself and think that God was going to come to my rescue once again and help me escape another dark and dreary storm in my life.

I went to Bible study one day, and a preacher of twenty years said, "No weapon that is formed against you shall prosper." I ran with it. It was a message from God. The LORD had sent me a word. Isaiah 54:17 became my favorite scripture. The government's witnesses were the weapons that would not prosper against me. Because the evidence that the government had against me only pertained to statements by other drug dealers, I said to myself, "Every tongue that should try to arise against me in judgment, God will condemn."

As my trial proceedings went forward, I kept in mind, "no weapon that is from against me shall prosper." I am a child of God now. God has forgiven me for all those things of my past. Therefore, the Lord will deliver me, and this shall come to pass also. God will allow me to come out on top. God is not going to let me go to prison. Me, me, me, me, me, me, me. It was all about me.

My trial ended in a hung jury. The jury could not reach a decision to unanimously find me guilty or not guilty. I did not have to go to prison, but I could not go home either. Deep down inside, I felt that I had won, but for some odd reason, I also had a feeling that my journey was far from over. I escaped a life sentence in federal prison that day. I was happy that the government's weapons did not prosper, and the tongues of all their witnesses who rose against me in judgment were condemned.

The government decided to take me to trial once again. This time, the government went out and found even more witnesses. Instead of getting better, my situation got much worse. Still, I held on to the word of God: "no weapon that is formed against me shall prosper, and every tongue that shall rise against me in judgment, God will condemn."

For three years, I fought against the federal government. After two years, I was tired of fighting, but I would not give up without a fight. I had become an avid reader and student of the Bible. Yes, I wanted to go free, but I also wanted to become a good servant of Jesus Christ. The spirit of the Lord was constantly teaching me so many things pertaining to God's word; therefore, doing God's will became the most important issue in my life. But when it came to my case, I was too far gone. I was indeed guilty, but I could not stop fighting for my freedom now. I needed God's help in choosing what I should do. I held on to God's word, "no weapon that is formed against me shall prosper; and every tongue that shall rise against me in judgment, God will condemn."

Ironically, God's help came in the form of one of the government's new star witnesses. This witness gave the government all that they needed to convict me. It was over. I could not go any farther. If I went to trial again, I would be convicted this time around. And being convicted meant that I would receive a life sentence in prison. The government's star witness became a weapon that could not be stopped.

This was the tongue that would tell it all. He was my brother. How could God allow this to happen to me? My brother was the help that God sent into my life in order to bring my battle with the government to an end. The government's weapon prospered against me, and the tongue that rose against me in judgment was not condemned. A very long prison sentence is all that greeted me at the end of my fight with the law.

I was sad because I realized that I would have to go to prison for many years. I was also sad and defeated because my brother was the weapon that the government used to convict me. I was also confused because I felt that the Bible had lied to me. All the government's weapons prospered, and the tongues(witnesses) that the government used against me were not condemned. I was very distraught. Giving up on all that the God had taught me was not an option, though. I pleaded guilty and did my best to accept my fate. I began to prepare my heart and mind for the long journey ahead.

* * *

It was all my fault I ended up having to go to prison for a very long time. It was not anyone else's fault, and it was certainly not my brother's fault. Although I wanted to point the finger at others and blame them for having to go to prison, it was my poor decisions in life and my own actions that slammed those iron bars behind me.

I pressed forward in my quest to become more familiar with the word of God. Everything happens for a reason, and I was certainly going to wrestle with God until he gave me a satisfying answer for the reason my situation turned out this way. I thought that my situation was ugly, but after further inspection, I realized that my soul was even uglier. God took his time before he revealed to me why my situation turned out to be such a mess. When God allowed me to see this awful mistake that I had made, I thanked him for saving me from a life sentence in prison.

"No weapon that is formed against thee shall prosper; and every tongue *that* shall rise against thee in judgment thou shalt condemn." This verse of the Bible had nothing to do with me overcoming the case that the government had against me nor with the tongues of those witnesses that testified against me. In fact, this Bible verse had nothing to do with any of my self-serving desires to win my freedom. The scripture of Isaiah 54:17 speaks exclusively concerning the hearts of obedient servants who believe in the truth of the New Testament and the many traditional belief systems that would challenge the righteousness of the New Testament. The weapons of the government should have prospered against me because my conduct as a Christian is not what the grand jury indicted me for. The charges against me that landed me in prison represented my own righteousness, not God's righteousness. My foolish imagination turned Isaiah 54:17 into a fairy tale script that would allow me to walk away from the charges against me unscathed.

The prophet Isaiah spoke these words almost a thousand years before Jesus was born. Once I realized this, God revealed to me that when the prophet Isaiah said that "No weapon that is formed against thee shall prosper; and every tongue *that* shall rise against thee in judgment thou shalt condemn . . . " Isaiah was speaking in terms of those who challenged the testimony of Jesus Christ not prospering. The traditional sculptured statues were the weapons(instruments) that the Gentiles would use to challenge the righteousness of Jesus Christ. The tongues that opposed Jesus Christ would be the words of those Jews and Gentiles who would rise against the saints of the New Testament as an adversary. It would be up to the saints to declare those things that opposed their faith to be fraudulent.

While I depended on the word of God to help me fight the government, I accepted the scriptures of the Bible completely out of context. I did not even research who the prophet Isaiah was, at what time in history Isaiah spoke these words, or who and what Isaiah was speaking about. Hearing the words "No weapon that is formed against thee shall prosper," I wanted these words to apply to my situation. I decided that God was speaking to me, and it almost cost me my life.

Everything that I needed to help me understand the true context of the scripture was right before my face. Before Isaiah wrote about no weapon prospering, Isaiah 54:15-16 says, "**Behold, they shall surely gather together, *but* not by me**(my righteous will)**: whosoever shall gather together against thee**(the righteousness of Jesus Christ)

shall fall(fail) **for thy**(Christ's) **sake. Behold, I have created the smith**(craftsman) **that bloweth the coals in the fire, and that bringeth forth an instrument**(weapon) **for his work; and I have created the waster**(corrupt thing) **to destroy**(pervert)."

The smith that blows the coals in the fire is the craftsman who uses their hands to create images of sculptured gods for people to worship, which in turn, became weapons that many people used to oppose the Christian disciples (Acts 19:23-27 / 2 Tim. 4:14-18). The "waster" is anyone who produces lies in order to pervert or oppose the truth of the gospel of Jesus Christ (Mat. 28:11-15 / Rom. 16:17-18 / 1 Cor. 1:12-17 / 10:12 / 2 Cor. 11:13-15 / Gal. 1:6-8 / Eph. 6:10-12 / Phi. 1:12-17 / Col. 2:8 / 1 Tim. 4:1-3 / 2 Tim. 4:3-4 / 2 Pet. 2:1-3 / 3 John 1:9-10 / Jude 1:16). These would be the weapons that would not prosper against the true believers. These would be the tongues that should rise against the spirit of Jesus Christ that dwells within the believers: the same tongues that the believers would have to condemn. Condemn how? By remaining faithful according to the example of Jesus Christ and not allowing perverted imitations of the gospel to move them away from the truth.

I thought the Bible lied to me because I ended up having to go to prison, but I lied to myself. The scripture was true. The mistake was that I applied the words of "No weapon that is formed against thee shall prosper" to a worldly situation: a situation that this verse should never have been used for. The situation that this verse applied to was my faith in Jesus Christ, my belief in God, and my efforts to sincerely obey the word of God according to the New Testament.

Weapons that people try to use to combat the truth of the gospel exist in various forms all throughout the world, including weapons that are formed by religious leaders who claim to belong to Christianity (Acts 20:28-30 / Jude 1:10-13). I allowed the weapon of perversion to be formed in my heart and prosper. I accepted a scripture out of context because of my desire to satisfy my personal situation rather than to obey God's will. The weapon of perversion prospered because it hindered me from receiving the true meaning of what the prophet Isaiah was saying in 54:17.

When it comes to those who oppose the believers within every day mundane situations, their weapons used to hinder us from achieving our desired goals will often prosper even if we are obedient Christians. But when it comes to our faith and our belief in the truth of God's will according to the New Testament, no weapon that is formed against the righteousness of Christ within our hearts shall prosper. Every tongue that rises against the righteousness of Christ within our hearts will be condemned through our example of obedience.

* * *

Many of the plots that people plan against us are mean-spirited and malicious, but this does not mean that God will not allow those mean-spirited weapons to prosper. Everything that we go through, God uses for us to grow thereby. God tests our reaction to all things and helps us to become more obedient in our decisions. Many awful things may prosper against us so that we can see the work of God taking place in our lives as we learn to forgive others and conform to the image of Jesus Christ.

The religious elite of Christ's era plotted to have him crucified. Did the efforts of the false witnesses who testified against Christ prosper? In the carnal aspect, yes, their efforts prospered. Although the false witnesses did not agree with one another, the fact that Jesus Christ was crucified showed that their tongues achieved success. They prospered in assisting in Christ's murder, but they failed to hinder Jesus Christ from obeying God's will. The religious elite succeeded in the carnal aspect of their weapons, prospering against Jesus Christ circumstantially. The same thing will indeed happen to us throughout our entire lives. There are certain things that God will not allow to happen for us. The people or the things that get in our way and hinder us from achieving our desired goals should not be referred to as the weapons and the tongues of Isaiah 54:17.

After the Jews succeeded in murdering Jesus, God raised him from the dead three days later. Because God raised Jesus Christ from the dead, his experience of being crucified on the cross should not be taken lightly.

Being nailed to the cross was a traumatic experience for Jesus. While on the cross, Jesus cried out shortly before his death, saying, "**My God, my God, why hast thou forsaken me** [Mat. 27:46]?" When individuals prosper in hindering our efforts to achieve a desired goal, we feel the same way Christ did. We feel that God has forsaken us and allowed the weapons of others to prosper against us.

Jesus Christ died on the cross. The Jews and the Gentiles that sought to destroy Jesus Christ succeeded, but their success only lasted for three days. God raised Jesus Christ from the dead as a sign of justification for all that Jesus Christ said and did. The Pharisees, the Sadducees, and all the other religious leaders of the Jews did not realize that the prophet Isaiah was speaking about their example of opposition to Christ's righteousness when he said, "**Behold, they shall surely gather together,** *but* **not by me**(God's righteous will)**: whosoever shall gather together against thee**(the righteousness of Christ) **shall fall**(fail) **for thy**(Christ's) **sake** [Isa. 54:15]." They failed to eliminate Jesus Christ. Because Jesus was successful in establishing the New Testament, God raised Jesus from the dead, and Christ's example of righteousness continues in the lives of his followers.

* * *

Moreover, what about the plight of Christ's apostles? The early Christian church of Jerusalem was scattered abroad because of the actions of Saul(Paul) after the Jews murdered a Christian named Stephen (Acts 8:1). Also, the Apostle James was killed by Herod in order to please the Jews (Acts 12:1-2). After Saul(Paul) believed in Jesus Christ, the Jews and the Gentiles chased him from villages, towns, cities, and countries nonstop (2 Cor. 11:21-33). Within each of these instances, the people who opposed the disciples of Jesus Christ prospered in their carnal efforts to harm or hinder them.

History tells us that the apostles Peter and Paul were murdered along with countless other Christians because of the righteousness of Jesus Christ that was within their hearts. The instruments of men as it pertains to individual plots to cause Christ's disciples harm physically, mentally, and emotionally are something that will always prosper from time to time. However, according to the New Testament, weapons of false religion and influences of hypocrisy will never prosper against Christians, who are the select few. Even within the religious world, the words and the voices that falsely represent the gospel will be shown to be false through our obedience.

For the first-generation saints, the gospel of Jesus Christ would be the new doctrine (Acts 17:16-20). It would be a strange thing: the newly formed religion, as some would consider it. All the other gods and all the other traditional religions of old had been around for hundreds of years. There was a point in history when the Egyptians dominated the world with their gods and customary religions (Jos. 24:14). Then came the Assyrians (2 Kings 17:6); then the Babylonians (Isa. 21:9); then the Medians and the Persians (Est. 1:3-4); then the Greeks (Joel 3:6), and finally the Romans with their multifaceted religious acceptance (John 11:48). All the kingdoms and empires had long ago introduced their belief systems to the world. The children of Israel also had their part in the historical order of religion by practicing the law of Moses among the Gentiles.

As the faith of the first-generation saints began to pick up speed, many challenged the validity of their belief system by comparing the ways of Jesus Christ to the traditional religions of old. Even the Jews, who believed in the coming of a Messiah, revolted against the disciples of Jesus Christ and challenged their faith.

* * *

In the second year of Christ's ministry, while in the city of Capernaum, the Jews questioned the words of Jesus. The previous day on the other side of the sea of Galilee, Jesus performed a miracle by feeding over five thousand people with only a small amount of bread and a few fish. The next morning, the crowd followed Jesus and his apostles across the sea to the city of Capernaum. When they asked Jesus how he came over the sea to this place, Jesus responded to them, saying, **"Verily, verily, I say unto you, Ye seek me, not because ye saw the miracles, but because** ye did eat of the loaves, and were filled. Labour not for the meat which perisheth, but for that meat which endureth unto everlasting life, which the Son of man shall give unto you: for him *hath* God the Father sealed** [John 6:26-27]."

Jesus proceeded to tell the people that he was the bread of life which came down from heaven, and that if they were to eat his flesh and drink his blood, they would live forever. Certain Jews that heard Jesus say these things considered him to be crazy or delusional. The people that Jesus spoke to were not strangers or foreigners. They were his kinfolk: those who had known him from his youth. Hearing Jesus say that he came from heaven confused the people, and they began to say among themselves, "**Is not this Jesus, the son of Joseph, whose father and mother we know? how is it then that he saith, I came down from heaven** [John 6:42]?"

Christ's physical appearance may have been produced by his mother, Mary, but the spiritual righteousness that he now displayed came from above. For the first thirty years of his life, Jesus represented Joseph, Mary, his brothers, and his sisters. But at the very instant he received the Holy Ghost, Jesus began to represent heaven. The son of Joseph that the Jews recognized was the outward appearance of Christ's bodily structure. The Son of God that Jesus was now claiming to be was the spirit that was now speaking to the Jews, saying, "**Verily, verily, I say unto you, Except ye eat**(receive) **the flesh**(example) **of the Son of man, and drink**(accept) **his blood**(spirit)**, ye have no life**(righteousness) **in you** [John 6:53]." Christ's words and his works are the part of Jesus that confirmed that he and God were one. These words and works began to manifest themselves only after Jesus received the Holy Spirit.

The Jews knew Jesus, the son of Mary and Joseph, but the Jews did not know Jesus Christ, the Son of God. Jesus knew what had taken place within him when he received the Holy Ghost, even if no one else knew what had taken place within him.

That day in the city of Capernaum, Jesus said to all that questioned his ministry, "**Murmur not among yourselves. No man can come to me, except the Father which hath sent me draw him: and I will raise him up at the last day. It is written in the prophets, And they shall** be all taught of God. Every man therefore that hath heard, and hath learned of the Father, cometh unto me [John 6:43-45]."

When Jesus Christ said to the Jews that "**No man can come to me, except the Father which *hath* sent me draw him** . . . **[John 6:44]**," at the same time, Jesus also said to them, "**It is written in the prophets, And they shall be all taught of God** [John 6:45]." Isaiah is the prophet who said that all the disciples of Jesus Christ would be taught of God. Jesus was quoting the Old Testament scripture of Isaiah 54:13 as he spoke to the people in order to bring context to what he was saying. In Isaiah 54:13, which is four verses before Isaiah said, "No weapon that is formed against thee shall prosper," he also said, "**And all thy children *shall be* taught of the LORD. . . .**"

One of the first weapons that the people tried to use against Jesus Christ was that they knew who he was. They knew his whole family; therefore, how could he come down from heaven? How could Jesus be the redeemer of Israel? They were missing the signs of the Messiah because they were focusing on his outward appearance. They closed their eyes to the works that Jesus Christ presented. The Jews did not want to accept that Jesus was their savior. His blessing of eternal life did not include fleshly benefits for them. When Jesus healed the blind man, the Pharisees did not want to accept that Jesus had performed such a miracle; therefore, they rebuked him and said, "**Thou art his disciple; but we are Moses' disciples. We know that God spake**(spoke) **unto Moses:** *as for* **this** *fellow,* **we know not from whence**(what source) **he is** [John 9:28-29]." Nevertheless, their efforts to hinder Christ did not prosper.

* * *

The Apostle Paul and the rest of the New Testament disciples also faced the weapons of those who opposed the righteousness of Jesus Christ. After Paul's first missionary journey, certain men came to the city of Antioch from Jerusalem and said to the believers, "**Except ye be circumcised after the manner**(example) **of Moses, ye cannot be saved [Acts 15:1].**" Paul and a disciple named Barnabas disputed with the men of Jerusalem because of this saying. Their attempt to turn the disciples away from the truth of the gospel was a weapon that would not prosper against the righteousness of Jesus Christ. Their words were the tongues that the apostles would have to condemn.

Because the men were from Jerusalem and because they said such things, they all decided to travel back to Jerusalem and speak with the elders of the church about this matter. Once they discussed it with the members of the church in Jerusalem, the Apostle Peter stood up and said, "**Men *and* brethren, ye know how that a good while ago God made choice among us, that the Gentiles by my mouth should hear the word of the gospel, and believe. And God, which knoweth the hearts, bare them**(the Gentiles) **witness, giving them the Holy Ghost, even as *he did* unto us**(the Jews)**; And put no difference between us**(Jews) **and them**(Gentiles)**, purifying their hearts by faith. Now therefore why tempt ye God, to put a yoke**(the law of Moses) **upon the neck**(will) **of the disciples, which neither our fathers nor we were able to bear? But we**(the Jews) **believe that through the grace of the Lord Jesus Christ we shall be saved, even as they**(the Gentiles) [Acts 15:7-11]." By these words, Peter confirmed Paul's argument. Regardless of what things may have been established in the past according to the law of Moses, the example of Jesus Christ will remain the truth of God's will from this point forward. As for the men of Jerusalem who came to Antioch and attempted to misdirect the disciple's faith, their weapon of perversion did not prosper, and their tongues that rose against the righteousness of Jesus Christ in judgment were condemned.

* * *

Furthermore, while Paul was in the city of Corinth, many of the Corinthians believed in the Lord Jesus Christ through Paul's preaching of the gospel. There were some that said they believed the gospel, but then they decided to twist the truth of the gospel and turn it into their own self-serving religious doctrines and belief systems. It came to pass that as they began to believe in Christ based on their own understanding, they also began to oppose Paul. Those who did not want to follow

Paul's directions in serving the Lord began to say such things as, "**For his**(*Paul's*) **letters . . . *are* weighty and powerful; but his**(*Paul's*) **bodily presence *is* weak, and his**(*Paul's*) **speech**(preaching) **contemptible** [2 Cor. 10:10]."

Pride and selfishness had found their way into the Corinthian body of believers, threatening to turn the truth of the gospel into evil and their lies into good. Many of the ministers in the Corinthian church had begun to measure themselves among themselves. Rather than build up and support the body of Christ, which they proudly claimed to be a part of, they began to question Paul's authority in the gospel and rose up against the things that had been previously taught by Paul. They confessed that they believed in Jesus Christ with their words, but they denied Christ's righteousness by the way they were choosing to serve Christ. They wanted to declare the good news of Jesus Christ based on their own thoughts and not according to the foundation that the Apostle Paul had already put in place for them to follow. Those who wanted to follow the gospel of Christ according to their own understanding became the weapon that would not prosper and the tongues that the disciples would have to condemn.

In Paul's second letter to the Corinthian church, he wrote to the believers in order to confirm and highlight the authority that the apostles received from God. The apostles received authority to set in place an orderly standard among the believers in order to help establish God's will according to the righteousness of Jesus Christ. As for the tongues that continued to rise up against the righteousness of Christ, Paul had this to say to them, "**Do ye look on things after the outward appearance? If any man trust to himself that he is Christ's, let him of himself think this again, that, as he *is* Christ's, even so *are* we**(the apostles) **Christ's. For though I should boast somewhat more of our**(the apostle's) **authority, which the Lord hath given us**(the apostles) **for edification, and not for your destruction, I should not be ashamed: That I may not seem as if I would terrify you by letters** [2 Cor. 10:7-9]."

There were those in the Corinthian church who acknowledged Jesus Christ, but at the same time, they began to imagine that gain was godliness. They wanted to lead before they even learned how to follow, thus becoming a weapon in opposition against the truth through their perverted efforts to declare the truth. They turned the battle towards one another as they went about to prove who could put on the best show of worshipping God in the name of Jesus Christ. They forgot that the war was against all imaginations and every high thought that exalts itself against the knowledge of God's will (2 Cor. 10:1-9).

The Corinthian's attempt to introduce carnal religion into the faith would not prosper against the sincere believers. The apostle's righteousness was of God. Therefore God confirmed the words of Isaiah, which say that "**. . . every tongue *that* shall rise against thee**(the righteousness of Jesus Christ) **in judgment thou**(the righteousness of Jesus Christ) **shalt condemn** [Isa. 54:17]." In the righteousness of Christ, Paul condemned the tongues of those who opposed him. Paul condemned those tongues by speaking, manifesting, and enduring in the truth of the gospel. This was Paul's heritage as a servant of God and as a child of God. Paul's efforts are also the example of our heritage as the children of God.

* * *

Our heritage, our righteousness, and our inheritance are to follow the righteousness of God according to the example of Jesus Christ (Matthew, Mark, Luke, and John) and the examples of his apostles (Acts through Revelation). Within the book of Isaiah, God was painting a metaphorical image of the body of Christ as he spoke through Isaiah. God used a symbolic dialect to describe the character of the New Testament saints that would reflect Christ's disciples. Speaking of those who mourn for righteousness and those who also seek comfort, Isaiah spoke a prophecy concerning the entrance of the new covenant, saying, "**O thou afflicted, tossed with the tempest, *and* not comforted, behold, I**(God) **will lay thy**(Christ's) **stones**(disciples) **with fair colours, and lay thy**(Christ's) **foundations**(disciples) **with sapphires. And I will make thy**(Christ's) **windows of agates, and thy**(Christ's) **gates of carbuncles, and all thy**(Christ's) **borders of** pleasant stones. And all thy(Christ's) children(disciples) *shall be* taught of the LORD; and great *shall be* the peace of thy(Christ's) children(disciples). In righteousness shalt thou(Christ) be established: thou(Christ) shalt be far from oppression; for thou(Christ) shalt not fear: and from terror; for it(fear and terror) shall not come near thee(Christ). Behold, they(those who oppose Christ) shall surely gather together, *but* not by me(God's righteous will): whosoever shall gather together against thee(the righteousness of Christ) shall fall(fail) for thy(Christ's) sake. Behold, I have created the smith(craftsmen) that bloweth the coals in the fire, and that bringeth forth an instrument(weapon) for his work; and I have created the waster(corrupt thing) to destroy(pervert). No weapon that is formed against thee(the righteousness of Christ) shall prosper; and every tongue(evil speaker) *that* shall rise against thee(the righteousness of Christ) in judgment thou(the righteousness of Christ) shalt condemn. This *is* the heritage of the servants of the LORD, and their righteousness *is* of me, saith the LORD [Isa. 54:11-17]."

As long as the first-generation saints followed in the footsteps of Jesus Christ, nothing that the people said could prosper against them in turning their hearts away from all that the Lord had taught them. The carnal desires of the Jews and Gentiles prospered in that they hunted the disciples, beat the disciples, disgraced the disciples, and they even killed many of the disciples. But their efforts to turn the disciples away from the truth of Jesus Christ did not prosper. The intentions of those who tried to influence the saints to give up on the testimony of Jesus Christ were the tongues that the disciples surely condemned.

The members of the body of Christ that are spread out all over the world at this present time in history face an even more burdensome task than that of the early saints. For two thousand years, man has attempted to recreate numerous versions of the gospel of Jesus Christ. The introduction of religious doctrines claiming to belong to the Christian faith has maliciously exploded on to the scene in the last century. Finding the true context of God's word has become a maze that is now accompanied by banners of strange teachings and symbols of deliberate carnal tampering. All these things and all the people who condone these things are the weapons and the tongues of Isaiah 54:17 that will not prosper against the elect children of God (Mat. 24:24,31).

Please, and I say again, please do not make the mistake of thinking that the scripture of Isaiah 54:17 is directed towards the everyday obstacles that arise in our lives, which may seem to hinder us from achieving our self-serving pleasures. If we are seeking a job and someone attempts to say or do things to hinder us, whatever methods they may use, please understand that it is not the weapon or the tongues of Isaiah 54:17. If we are seeking a wife, a husband, a bank loan, a promotion, or even our freedom from prison and someone seems to do or say something that hinders the process, please understand that whatever they say or do, their actions does not represent the weapons and the tongues of Isaiah 54:17. However, if someone says something that is contrary to the truth of the gospel of Jesus Christ, in an attempt to divert us from striving for the truth of God's will, they have now become the weapon and the tongue which shall not prosper against the righteousness of Jesus Christ within us. If someone attempts to hinder you from walking in Christ's righteousness, they have then become the weapon and the tongue, which shall not prosper against the righteousness of Jesus Christ within us.

We are commanded by God to examine our souls every hour of the day, whether times are good or bad. Fairy tale edification is a familiar weapon that many will use to move us away from the truth of Jesus Christ. Sometimes our own delusional mental state accepts the scriptures out of context, which leads us to think that the scriptures mean one thing when in truth, the scriptures signify something totally different. Imaginary teachings that stimulate emotions will be the tongues that we must be in a hurry to condemn. We are taught to stand strong and remain faithful to the example of the apostles of Christ. As for all the leaders and the ministers who neglected to follow Paul's lead as he preached the truth, Paul tagged them with this label, saying, "**For such *are* false apostles, deceitful workers, transforming themselves into the apostles of Christ. And no marvel; for Satan himself is transformed into an angel**(messenger) **of light**(truth)**. Therefore *it is***

no great thing if his ministers(weapons) **also be transformed as the ministers of righteousness; whose end shall be according to their works** [2 Cor. 11:13-15]."

Understand the word of God and believe the word of God, but most of all, trust in the true context of the word of God concerning how we must believe in Jesus Christ. Then and only then, no tradition, no religion, and no carefully crafted belief system of man will prosper against us, for we will condemn all the voices of opposition that rise up against us as an adversary. We will declare all the historical instruments of the familiar religions to be wrong and unfit in the sight of God. This is our heritage, and our righteousness is of the LORD. No weapon that is formed against thee shall prosper has just been revealed in Divine Context.

∙ ∙

Context #14 reveals how the New Testament is the covenant that God made with all nations and all races.

∙ ∙

HOSEA 2:18

18. And in that day will I make a covenant for them with the beasts of the field and with the fowls of heaven, and *with* the creeping things of the ground: and I will break the bow and the sword and the battle out of the earth, and will make them to lie down safely.

The Covenant With The Beasts, With The Fowls, And With The Creeping Things

Divine Context is understanding that when God spoke through the prophet Hosea saying that he would ". . . make a covenant for them with the beasts of the field, and with the fowls of heaven, and *with* the creeping things of the ground . . . ," God was not referring to the animal kingdom. The covenant with the beasts, with the fowls, and with the creeping things is the covenant of grace that God made with the Gentile population through the testimony of Jesus Christ.

* * *

The state of mankind without the presence of God reveals that humans are just as much a part of the animal kingdom as the wild untamed beasts of the fields. Mankind was once thought of as cavemen: brute beasts that clubbed the woman of his desires over the head as a show of intimacy and ran around crouched over like apes battling with wild animals in competition for food.

Of course, this is all assumed through scientific research. Much of these assumptions come from historical findings and the ongoing observation of the tribal men and women that are tucked off in some of the most remote corners of the earth, far removed from modern civilizations. The way these ancient cultures hunted, prepared their food, and socialized gives us an image of the state of man in the stages of our early development.

There are people on earth right now who live their entire lives without seeing or driving a motor vehicle, listening to a radio, or experiencing the convenience or the sanitation of a conventional toilet stool. These are the people that many call dumb and ignorant. There are those who look down on them as if these less modernized individuals are uncivilized or savages. What we must recognize is that without the truth of Jesus Christ in our lives, we who inhabit the modernized world are just the same as they are, if not worse. Without the testimony of Jesus Christ in our lives, we all bear the image of untamed beasts.

The information age tends to make everyone forget about how uncivilized the human condition has always been. Even now, the world remains filled with savagery and carnage. Only now, it is muffled by the overwhelming majority who search for excuses rather than reasons. The political correctness of the free world leads us to believe that all of mankind is civil, reasonable, and rational. The honesty of man's state teaches us that without the grace of God, even the most intelligent human beings still bear the instincts of a wild animal. How many of us do things that we do not desire to do? And of the things that we desire to do continually, how often do we fall short? The beast is always alive within us, even when God's wisdom is present.

King Solomon was said to be the wisest man the world had ever seen. People traveled from distant countries to hear Solomon speak. Solomon was not only wise, but at that present time in history, he was also the richest king that the world had ever seen. In his wisdom, Solomon indulged in many abominable practices that were condemned by God. Yes, the very same God that had given Solomon the wisdom that others coveted, cherished, and idolized. Solomon indulged in whatever his heart desired. Of the three books that are said to be authored by Solomon, the book of Ecclesiastes reveals the most about Solomon's mental state.

The Covenant With The Beasts, With The Fowls

Vanity is the subject matter of the book of Ecclesiastes. Therein Solomon speaks of the sorrows of wisdom and the vexation that his heart experienced as he searched for the pleasures of all that the world has to offer the human soul. In a certain portion of Ecclesiastes, Solomon gives his thoughts on the fate of human beings in comparison to the fate of untamed animals, saying, "**I said in my heart concerning the estate**(order) **of the sons of men, that God might manifest**(cleanse) **them, and that they might see that they themselves are beasts. For that which befalleth the sons of men befalleth beasts; even one thing befalleth them: as the one dieth, so dieth the other; yea, they have all one breath; so that a man hath no preeminence**(profit) **above a beast: for all *is* vanity. All go unto one place; all are of the dust, and all turn to dust again. Who knoweth the spirit of man that goeth upward, and the spirit of the beast that goest downward to the earth? Wherefore I perceive that *there is* nothing better, than that a man should rejoice in his own works; for that *is* his portion: for who shall bring him to see what shall be after him** [Ecc. 3:18-22]?"

Herein lies the problem. When we concentrate solely on rejoicing in our own works, we are servants to ourselves. Pride, carnal wisdom, and narcissism can have this effect on the human psyche, revealing that our natural instincts are no different than that of beasts.

* * *

Approximately fourteen hundred years before God made his covenant with the beasts, the fowls, and the creeping things of the ground, God separated a group of people of the same family and called them his holy nation (Exo. 19:5-6). All other people who were not a part of this family were considered unclean and common. Another title that was given to all those outside of God's holy nation was Gentiles (Judg. 4:1-2). While God's nation enjoyed the intimacy of knowing firsthand who and what God was, the Gentiles remained fish out of water, flapping and flailing from generation to generation, claiming almost anything to be their god in hopes of finding a revelation that would give them direction and reveal the true purpose of life here on earth.

The people of the holy nation that God separated for himself were called Israelites (Exo. 9:7 / Lev. 23:42-43). The Israelites knew God, and most importantly, the Israelites knew what was expected of them according to God's will. While the rest of the world embraced imaginary faith, the people of Israel experienced the intimacy that other nations had no idea could exist between the Creator and mortal man. Without God's presence among the Israelites, they were no different than all the other nations on earth. Even with God's presence among them, the Israelites still showed themselves to be dominated by the urge to run wild and manifest their kinship to the Gentile world by worshiping anything and everything, including the domesticated cattle of the field (Exo. 32:1-6).

Although the Israelites were chosen to be God's people, they would only be special above all other races for a limited time. They were chosen to be God's people for one reason. God would preserve their bloodline so that all other races could one day receive the grace of God, also. Yes, the Israelite family was given the benefits of knowing God long before the Gentiles, but it is evident that God was going to bring their boasting to an end. God spoke to the forefather of the Israelite family tree, saying, "**. . . in thee and in thy seed shall all the families**(Gentiles) **of the earth be blessed** [Gen. 28:14]." Abraham, Isaac, and Jacob (Israel) were the father, son, and grandson who God used to reveal his plans of the mercy that would one day be available for every human being, whether they were an Israelite or a Gentile (Gen. 22:15-18/26:1-5/28:10-15).

The fulfillment of all the families of the earth being blessed through Jacob's seed would be God's covenant with the beasts, the fowls, and the creeping things. Hearing that God was making a covenant with the beasts of the field, our carnal thoughts can lead us to believe that God was going to make a covenant with the animal kingdom. Animals are unique in their own special way. Instinctively animals do exactly what they are created to do. But the covenant that the prophet Hosea spoke of would indeed be a covenant with the Gentile population of the world.

Hosea was an Israelite who lived and prophesied during a time of turmoil and idolatry. Idolatry is the worshipping of anyone or anything above God's commandments or the worshipping of anything along

The Covenant With The Beasts, With The Fowls 215

with God's commandments that have not been authorized by the will of God. The people of Israel had been separated into two different kingdoms long before God called Hosea to be a prophet. Because Solomon worshipped idols during his time as king over God's people, God divided the kingdom of Israel in two, giving ten tribes to be ruled by Jeroboam of the tribe of Ephraim and two tribes to be ruled by the sons of king David (1 Kings 11:29-33).

Once God divided the people of Israel into two separate kingdoms, Jeroboam the king of the northern kingdom, began to think that when all the people of Israel would return to Jerusalem every year for the customary feasts, they would eventually turn their hearts back to the sons of David and forsake him. Therefore, Jeroboam made two golden calves for the people of the northern kingdom to worship as their gods. In his fear, Jeroboam appointed priests that were not ordained by God to minister to the people of Israel (1 Kings 12:25-31). Therefore, the book of Hosea speaks of whoredom and how the people of Israel worshiped idols rather than God. God would eventually destroy the entire northern kingdom of Israel, but before doing so, he inspired Hosea to declare the covenant that he would make with the Gentiles.

Around one hundred and eighty years after the northern kingdom of Israel was formed, the prophet Hosea arrived on the scene, speaking the word of the LORD. The bulk of Hosea's words are directed towards the northern kingdom of Israel; nevertheless, comments concerning the southern kingdom of Judah can be found throughout Hosea's prophecy. Forty years after God called Hosea to be a prophet, the Assyrian king Shalmaneser came and destroyed the entire northern kingdom of Israel. The king of Assyria scattered the inhabitants of the northern kingdom all throughout the land among the Gentile nations that they once despised. Jerusalem and the southern kingdom of Israel survived the onslaught of Assyria and would remain a nation for almost one hundred and fifty more years until the Babylonian king Nebuchadnezzar came and destroyed their capital city Jerusalem.

Once the northern kingdom of Israel was destroyed, the Gentiles that the Assyrian king brought in from other countries began to mix with the Israelites who remained in the land. Eventually, this half-breed race became Samaritans (2 Kings 17:29). Samaritans were a cross between an Israelite and a Gentile, a racial hybrid, so to speak. The remaining two tribes of Judah and Benjamin began to look down on the Samaritans and would not acknowledge them as their kindred. The Samaritans became an abomination in the eyes of the people of Judah, and they refused to have anything to do with them.

The people of Judah were only following a commandment that was given to them by Moses, which commanded the Israelites not to cohabitate with other races or nationalities (Deu. 7:1-6). This is evident in the gospel, according to John. When Jesus spoke to a woman who was a Samaritan, the woman responded to Jesus by saying, "**How is it that thou, being a Jew, askest drink of me, which am a woman of Samaria** [John 4:9]?" The scripture then goes on to say, "**. . . for the Jews have no dealings with the Samaritans** [John 4:9]."

Because the Samaritans were half Israelite and half Gentile, an awkward development sprung up in the order of those who had and those who had not. The Jews were God's holy people; they were "the haves." The Gentiles, on the other hand, were the uncivilized heathens because they had no idea who the LORD was; they were "the have nots." And then came the Samaritans. They did not authentically belong on either side of the fence. Nevertheless, scripture shows that the Samaritans claimed the same belief system as the people of Israel (John 4:11-12).

The prophet Hosea made this distinction when he spoke of how God was going to destroy the northern kingdom of Israel and scatter the ten tribes among the Gentiles. This would result in those ten tribes being mixed with the Gentiles, thus becoming the Samaritans (Hos. 1:4). Hosea also spoke about how God would protect the two tribes of the southern kingdom of Israel, Judah and Benjamin (Hos.1:6-7). Hosea then spoke of how God would one day adopt the Gentiles that were not his people. When God spoke of the Gentile population of the world that had no idea who the living God was, Hosea said, "**Call his**(the Gentiles) **name Loammi: for ye**(the Gentiles) ***are* not my people, and I will not be your *God*. Yet the number of the children of Israel shall be as the sand of the sea, which cannot be measured nor numbered; and it shall come to pass, *that* in the place where it was said unto them**(the

Gentiles), **Ye *are* not my people, *there* it shall be said unto them**(the Gentiles), **Ye *are* the sons of the living God** [Hos. 1:9-10]."

The beasts, the fowls, and the creeping things would finally get their chance to know the living God. The Israelites held a major advantage above all other nations because they had already known the living God for over fifteen hundred years. Now, the Gentiles would receive the opportunity to also be called God's people. Nevertheless, the Israelites, the tribes of Judah and Benjamin, to be exact, were not going to be forgotten by God. The Israelites would automatically be welcomed into God's new world order, but with exceptions. The pure bloodline Israelites would have to set their "king of the jungle" mentality aside and believe in Jesus Christ if they still desired to be called the people of God (Rom. 9:1-8).

* * *

After the prophet Hosea spoke his prophetic words to the children of Israel, over five hundred years came and went before the first glimmer of hope for the Gentiles began to show itself. However, the covenant with the beasts of the field did not appear to be valid in the beginning. As Jesus began to speak the gospel of the new covenant, he seemed to exclude the Gentiles and the Samaritans. When Jesus first chose his twelve apostles to go out and prepare the people of the world for his arrival, he spoke to his apostles, saying, "**Go not into the way of the Gentiles, and into *any* city of the Samaritans enter ye not: But go rather to the lost sheep of the house of Israel** [Mat. 10:5-6]." Whoa! What about the Gentiles and the Samaritans? Were they unfit to receive the grace of God? Did they not deserve the chance to receive the mercy promised to them by God?

Let us not get ahead of ourselves by thinking that God would exclude the Gentiles and the Samaritans from his grace. When Jesus Christ told his apostles to go out and seek only the lost sheep of the house of Israel, this was not about God once again rejecting the Gentiles or the Samaritans. Sending the apostles to the lost sheep of the house of Israel was God's way of first establishing the appearance of the Messiah among those who were most familiar with the Messiah's documented attributes.

The Gentile population of the world was not looking for a Savior. And the Samaritan population of the world had become so engulfed with pagan religion and Gentile philosophy that their thoughts towards the Messiah was stagnated. Jesus wanted to saturate the Israelite(Jewish) population with the fulfillment of the long-awaited promise and then allow the rest of the world to climb aboard as the momentum of the new covenant picked up speed.

The works of God's covenant with the beasts of the field included the testimony of Jesus Christ. After three years of wrestling with the hierarchy of the Jewish leaders, Jesus was finally beaten and hung on a tree. The religious elite enjoyed their victory as Jesus Christ gave up the ghost. What they did not know was that Christ's death on the cross was all a part of God's mysterious plan. Three days after giving up the ghost, God justifiably raised Jesus from the dead, and Jesus showed himself to the apostles who would carry his legacy out into the world.

One of the individuals who communed with Jesus after God raised him from the dead was the Apostle Peter. Peter was an Israelite and a very obedient servant to the Old Testament law of Moses. When Jesus first began to preach the New Testament, one of the first individuals he chose to be a part of his ministry was Peter. Jesus said to Peter and his brother Andrew that he would make them fishers of men (Mat. 4:19). Peter became someone who witnessed all the words and all the works of Jesus Christ. Once Jesus was raised from the grave, Jesus communed with all his apostles except for Judas, who had betrayed him. Shortly before Jesus was taken up into heaven by a cloud, he told his apostles that "**. . . they should not depart from Jerusalem, but wait for the promise of the Father, which,** *saith he,* **ye have heard of me** [Acts 1:4]." At this same time, Jesus also spoke to the apostles, saying, "**For John** (the Baptist) **truly baptized with water; but ye shall be baptized with the Holy Ghost not many days hence** [Acts 1:5]."

According to the history of the Israelites, it was written that a great king of the seed of David would restore the Israelites back into an independent nation far removed from being ruled and dominated by the Gentile kingdoms of the world. Because of these sayings, Christ's

The Covenant With The Beasts, With The Fowls 219

apostles asked him if he would restore the kingdom of Israel at this time. Therefore, Jesus said to them, "**It is not for you to know the times or the seasons, which the Father hath put in his own power. But ye shall receive power**(ability)**, after that the Holy Ghost is come upon you: and ye shall be witnesses unto me both in Jerusalem, and in all Judaea**(the Jews)**, and in Samaria**(the Samaritans)**, and unto the uttermost**(Gentile) **part of the earth** [Acts 1:7-8]."

Ten days after Jesus spoke these words to his apostles, informing them that they would gain power after they received the Holy Ghost, that is exactly what happened. As all the apostles were gathered in Jerusalem on the day of Pentecost, the Holy Ghost came on each of them. The Apostle Peter began to quote the Old Testament prophet, Joel, saying to all the Jews in Jerusalem that the promise of the Messiah had arrived (Joel 2:28-29). When certain Jews heard Peter speaking concerning the new covenant, they thought that Peter was drunk. But there were others who joyfully welcomed the words of Peter and became followers of Jesus Christ (Acts 2:40-42).

Once the apostles of Jesus began to spread the gospel among the Jews day after day, the Jews who did not believe the gospel began to persecute those who did believe. Therefore, many of the disciples fled from Jerusalem. A disciple named Philip fled from Jerusalem and came to a city of the Samaritans and began to preach the gospel to them. Before Philip came to the city of the Samaritans preaching the gospel, the ministers of Christ remained in Jerusalem, preaching to none other than the Jews. To go out and speak of Jesus to others was risky and brought with it the possibility of rejection and even physical harm. But through the grace of God, many of the Samaritans believed in Jesus Christ after hearing the words of Philip.

Word spread fast about how the Samaritans had accepted the gospel of Jesus Christ. And when the apostles Peter and John came to the city of the Samaritans, they prayed for them, and they received the Holy Ghost (Acts 8:14-17). For the Samaritans to believe in Jesus Christ was surprising, but it was not a stretch. The Samaritans were very familiar with the promises of Israel. Although the Samaritans were half Gentile, they were also half Israelite; therefore, they felt somewhat obligated to the promise, which they assumed partly belonged to them also. Introducing Jesus Christ to the full-blooded Gentiles would be another battle altogether for the apostles, but the battle was already won.

Once things settled down in Jerusalem, Peter went and communed with the disciples in the city of Lydda. Peter healed a man that was sick; therefore, when they of the nearby city of Joppa heard that Peter was in Lydda, they sent for Peter to come and see a disciple named Tabitha, who had been sick and had recently died. Peter then went to Joppa, and God allowed Peter to raise Tabitha back to life.

While Peter remained in the city of Joppa with the disciples, God appeared to a Gentile named Cornelius in the city of Caesarea. In the vision, an angel of God said to Cornelius, "**Thy prayers and thine alms**(good deeds) **are come up for a memorial before God. And now send men to Joppa, and call for** *one* **Simon, whose surname**(family name) **is Peter: He lodgeth with one Simon a tanner, whose house is by the sea side: he shall tell thee what thou oughtest to do** [Acts 10:4-6]."

The day after Cornelius received the vision from God, he sent his servants to the city of Joppa to look for Peter. As Cornelius' servants were on their way to Joppa to find Peter, Peter went up on the roof of the house to pray. While Peter was on the roof waiting for dinner to be served, he became hungry and fell into a trance. A vision then appeared to Peter. The scripture says that while Peter was in a trance, he "**. . . saw heaven opened, and a certain vessel descending unto him, as it had been a great sheet knit**(secured) **at the four corners, and let down to the earth: Wherein were all manner of fourfooted beasts of the earth, and wild beasts, and creeping things, and fowls of the air. And there came a voice to him, Rise, Peter; kill, and eat. But Peter said, Not so, Lord; for I have never eaten anything that is common or unclean. And the voice** *spake* **unto him again the second time, What God hath cleansed,** *that* **call not thou common. This was done thrice**(three times)**: and the vessel was received up again into heaven** [Acts 10:11-16]." Peter doubted in himself what this vision could mean. According to the Old Testament law, the Israelites were commanded by God not to eat certain animals. In fact, those who did eat an unclean animal or even touched an unclean animal were unclean according to Old Testament law (Lev. 5:2).

The vision that Peter received was an indirect message from God, and it would not be long before Peter realized this. While Peter gave thought to what the vision should mean, the servants of Cornelius stood at the gate of the house asking for Peter. Then the Holy Ghost said to Peter, "**Behold, three men seek thee. Arise therefore, and get thee down, and go with them, doubting nothing: for I have sent them** [Acts 10:19-20]." The next day Peter went with the men back to the city of Caesarea, where Cornelius was. When they arrived in the city of Caesarea, Cornelius, along with his family members and close friends, were gathered to greet Peter.

As Peter entered the house, Cornelius fell at his feet to worship him. But Peter stopped Cornelius from doing such a thing, saying, "**Stand up; I myself also am a man** [Acts 10:26]." Peter also reminded the Gentiles about the principles of the Old Testament, saying, "**Ye know how that it is an unlawful thing for a man that is a Jew to keep company**(fellowship), **or come unto**(visit) **one of another nation**(race)**; but God hath shewed me** (in a vision) **that I should not call any man**(Gentile) **common or unclean. Therefore came I *unto you* without gainsaying**(hesitating)**, as soon as I was sent for: I ask therefore for what intent ye have sent for me** [Acts 10:28-29]?" Cornelius then told Peter about the vision that he received from God.

After Peter understood why Cornelius had sent for him, he began to preach the gospel of Jesus to them, saying, "**Of a truth I perceive that God is no respecter of persons: But in every nation he that feareth him**(God)**, and worketh righteousness, is accepted with him**(God)**. The word which *God* sent unto the children of Israel, preaching peace by Jesus Christ: (he is Lord of all:) That word, *I say*, ye know, which was published throughout all Judaea, and began from Galilee, after the baptism which John** (the Baptist) **preached: How God anointed Jesus of Nazareth with the Holy Ghost and with power: who went about doing good, and healing all that were oppressed of the devil; for God was with him. And we**(the apostles) **are witnesses of all things which he did both in the land of the Jews,** and in Jerusalem; whom they slew(killed) and hanged on a tree(cross): Him God raised up the third day, and shewed him openly; Not to all the people, but unto witnesses chosen before of God, *even to us*(the apostles), who did eat and drink with him after he rose from the dead. And he commanded us(the apostles) to preach unto the people, and to testify that it is he which was ordained of God *to be* the Judge of quick(the saved) and dead(the unsaved). To him give all the prophets** (of the Old Testament) **witness, that through his name whosoever believeth in him shall receive remission of sins. While Peter yet spake these words, the Holy Ghost fell on all them**(the Gentiles)** which heard(understood) the word. And they of the circumcision(Jews) which believed were astonished, as many as came with Peter, because that on the Gentiles also was poured out the gift of the Holy Ghost** [Acts 10:34-45]."

The Jews that came to Cornelius' house with Peter were surprised to see that God would also allow the Gentiles to receive the gift of the new covenant. The Gentiles were unlearned, uncivilized, and heathens of the earth. The Gentiles were those who the Jews were taught never to keep company with because they were common and unclean. Finally, the Gentiles had become the beasts of the field, the fowls of the air, and the creeping things of the ground to whom God had introduced himself. The prophet Hosea spoke the words, Peter saw the vision, and God fulfilled the covenant by pouring the Holy Ghost into the hearts of the beasts, the fowls, and the creeping things. The truth of the new covenant was now revealing itself. The Gentiles would now reap the benefits of the long-awaited Messiah.

All of mankind now had the chance to stand on equal footing before God. There was no such thing as an Israelite, a Samaritan, or a Gentile in the righteousness of Jesus Christ. There were only the believers and the unbelievers. But everyone was not happy about God having mercy on the Gentiles. The Jews had to humble themselves and relinquish their title of being God's special people and face the fact that they were now no different than a Gentile or a Samaritan in the eyes of God. That title now belonged to those who would receive Jesus Christ as their Lord and Savior. The only advantage that a Jew held over a Gentile in the body of

The Covenant With The Beasts, With The Fowls

Christ was that a Jew would be much more familiar with the promises of the new covenant based solely on their cultural upbringing (Rom. 3:1-2).

When Peter arrived back in Jerusalem, there were certain Jews who confronted Peter, saying, "**Thou wentest in to men uncircumcised**(the Gentiles)**, and didst eat**(fellowship) **with them** [Acts 11:3]." Peter defended himself and told them about the vision of the beasts of the earth, the creeping things, and the fowls of the air. Peter also told them how Cornelius had sent to Joppa for him and that as he spoke to the Gentiles, they received the Holy Ghost in the same manner that they all received the Holy Ghost on the day of Pentecost. After explaining to the Jews what happened while he preached the word of God to the Gentiles, Peter concluded his argument, saying, "**Then remembered I the word of the Lord, how that he said, John** (the Baptist) **indeed baptized with water; but ye shall be baptized with the Holy Ghost. Forasmuch then as God gave them**(the Gentiles) **the like gift as** *he did* **unto us, who believed on the Lord Jesus Christ; what was I, that I could withstand God** [Acts 11:16-17]?" When the Jews heard everything that Peter said, they held their peace and glorified God, saying, "**Then hath God also to the Gentiles granted repentance unto life** [Acts 11:18]."

Peter was an apostle, and Peter was responsible for the distribution of the gospel. Peter knew that he could not discriminate against the Gentiles, no matter how much the other Jews disliked the idea of him speaking to them concerning the gospel of Jesus Christ. It was God's grace, and whoever God chose to give his gift to, no human being had the power to oppose God successfully. Peter knew about God's covenant with the beasts, the fowls, and the creeping things. Yes, God showed Peter the vision while he was in a trance on the roof, but the vision was only a confirmation of what the prophet Hosea had already spoken about long ago.

* * *

Hosea's prophecy is littered with God's anger towards the idolatry(whoredom) of his people of old. Generation after generation, the Israelites moved farther and farther away from the law that God had ordained for them. Punishment had to be rendered. God's vengeance was recognized when he allowed the Assyrians to destroy the northern kingdom of Israel. But God is also merciful; therefore, God set a silver lining within all the sorrow that was to come on the northern kingdom of Israel.

Not even knowing at what time or exactly when this covenant would be fulfilled, as a faithful servant Hosea spoke what the Holy Ghost had revealed to him, saying, "**Therefore, behold, I**(God) **will allure her**(the Israelites)**, and bring her into the wilderness, and speak comfortably unto her. And I**(God) **will give her**(the Israelites) **her vineyards from thence, and the valley of Achor for a door of hope: and she**(the Israelites) **shall sing there, as in the days of her youth, and as in the day when she came up out of the land of Egypt**(bondage)**. And it shall be at that day, saith the LORD,** *that* **thou shalt call me Ishi**(my husband)**; and shalt call me no more Baali**(my master)**. For I will take away the names of Baalim**(the pagan gods) **out of her**(Israel's) **mouth, and they**(the pagan gods) **shall no more be remembered by their name. And in that day will I make a covenant for them with the beasts of the field and with the fowls of heaven, and** *with* **the creeping things of the ground: and I will break**(destroy) **the bow and the sword and the battle**(controversy of who God truly is) **out of the earth, and will make them to lie down safely. And I will betroth**(engage) **thee**(the Jewish believers) **unto me for ever; yea, I will betroth thee unto me in righteousness, and in judgment, and in lovingkindness, and in mercies. I will even betroth thee unto me in faithfulness: and thou shalt know the LORD. And it shall come to pass in that day, I will hear, saith the LORD, I will hear**(bear witness to) **the heavens**(Old Testament prophesies)**, and they**(the prophecies) **shall hear**(begin to testify unto) **the earth**(the believers)**; And the earth**(the believers) **shall hear**(respond to) **the corn**(word of God)**, and the wine**(the Spirit of God)**, and the oil**(understanding of the word)**; and they**(the Gentiles) **shall hear**(sing together with) **Jezreel**(the Israelites)**. And I will sow her**(the Gentiles) **unto me in the earth; and I will have mercy upon her**(the Gentiles) **that had not obtained mercy; and I will say to

The Covenant With The Beasts, With The Fowls

them*(the Gentiles)* **which were not my people, Thou**(The Gentiles who believe) ***art(are)*** **my people; and they**(the Gentiles who believe) **shall say, *Thou art* my God** [Hos. 2:14-23]."

In Peter's first general letter to the Christian population of the world, he wrote of how the testimony of Jesus Christ was a stumbling stone to the unbelieving Jews (1 Pet. 2:7-8). Then Peter wrote concerning the Gentiles who believed in Jesus, saying, "**But ye *are* a chosen generation, a royal priesthood, an holy nation, a peculiar people; that ye should shew forth the praises of him**(God) **who hath called you out of darkness into his marvellous light: Which in time past *were* not a people, but *are* now the people of God: which had not obtained mercy, but now have obtained mercy** [1 Pet. 2:9-10]." The words documented within Peter's first letter contain the direct quote from the book of Hosea. Peter was no stranger to the promise of the Holy Ghost being shed on all the individuals who God had predestinated to receive eternal life, whether they were an Israelite, a Samaritan, or a Gentile.

* * *

The tug of war concerning who belongs to God still exists between the Jews and the Gentiles even two thousand years after Jesus Christ settled the matter. According to the new covenant of Jesus Christ, God does not care about what race we are. All that matters to God is an open and obedient heart that is willing to accept and obey the gospel of Jesus Christ. Peter, who was a witness and trusted servant of the Lord, said to Cornelius, "**Of a truth I perceive that God is no respecter of persons: But in every nation**(race) **he that feareth him**(God)**, and worketh righteousness, is accepted with him** [Acts 10:34-35]." This is the important element of the new covenant that we all must focus on.

The covenant of God's new generation is blind to all the man-made religions that categorize us by our color, our kindred, our wealth, or even by our education. The God we serve is amazingly mysterious in how he declares the heavenly dialect that relays his message to humans (1 Cor. 2:6-8). With all the technology that surrounds us, regardless of how much we know and no matter who we are descendants of, if we think that our wisdom of God is of ourselves, then we are willfully ignorant. As king Solomon says, without a clean heart, mankind has no benefit above the animals of the earth (Ecc. 3:19).

For over fourteen hundred years, God preserved a particular race of people, so that every other race on earth could one day receive the opportunity to understand the intimacy that God offers to the entire human race. All those races outside of the Israelites lived in ignorance with no hope of finding out who the living God truly is (Eph. 2:11-13). Does this mean that the Gentiles were the race whose forefathers were the cavemen of fictional tales, the cannibals of the lost worlds, or even the slaves who once served the mighty and the powerful? Thanks to God, it does not even matter anymore because the covenant with the beasts, with the fowls, and with the creeping things offers the same weight in glory as the new covenant with the Israelites. Within the new covenant, they are both one in the same (Gal. 3:27-29).

Jews, Samaritans, and Gentiles are made one through the mercy of God. Now the Gentile does not have a reason to look up to the Jew. Neither does the Jew have a reason to look down on the Gentile. The body of Christ bears the scars of all races, all nationalities, and all cultures. There is not one race that is special above another race in Christ. There is one Lord: the Lord Jesus Christ. There is one faith that we are all justified thereby: the faith of the Lord Jesus Christ. And there is one God: the Father of our Lord and Savior Jesus Christ.

Through the power and wisdom of God, the Gentile population of the earth has been given a chance to rise and stand on the same stage as the Jews who have received the gift of the new covenant. The Gentiles have been transformed from the beasts of the field to brothers of favor, from fowls of the air to faithful saints who care, and from creeping things of the ground to willing servants of God who abound. It is our God that does these things for mankind. Our God fulfills his word in order to reconstruct the heart and bring balance to the scales of the conscience. Let all the creatures of divine intelligence look to God and be thankful for the gift of the Holy Ghost that God has graciously poured on us because we are no more what we once were in his sight.

Believe in God, and have faith in Jesus Christ, my fellow brothers and sisters; understand that no matter what nationality or culture we were born into, we now all belong to the New Covenant through God's gift of the Holy Ghost. God speed. The covenant with the beasts, the fowls, and the creeping things has just been revealed in Divine Context.

Epilogue

My earnest desire is for those who read this book to examine, inspect, and consider all that is declared and proposed therein. Whether you accept the revelations of DIVINE CONTEXT (Vol. 1) or not, the critical thought process of examination dwells within the conscious of us all. To exercise your critical thought process is a right through the liberty of independence that has been freely given to us by the grace of individuality.

There will be certain individuals who will deny, reject, and oppose the words of this book. All I ask you to do is remember this one thing: truth in its most sincere form should always be the goal of the reader. Divine truth is complete truth; otherwise, the word of God and the interpretation of God's word becomes a harmful object in the imaginations of wolves in sheep's clothing. It is much easier for us to either accept or reject what someone says rather than examine what someone says. Please examine the scriptures continually with a sincere heart, my fellow believers. Never forget, "**. . . faith without works is dead** [Jam. 2:20]?" God speed!

About the Author

Angelo was born and raised in Lake Placid, Florida. He graduated from Lake Placid High in 1991. Angelo holds an Associates of Arts and Biblical Studies degree from Belhaven University and lives in the Orlando Florida area with his wife, Tamekia. They have 8 children and 12 wonderful grandchildren. Angelo was called into the ministry in 1999. For the last 24 years, he has dedicated his time and efforts to teaching Christians the true context of God's holy word. Called by God to teach the word, Angelo believes that in order to truly understand our relationship with God, we must first understand the true context of God's holy word.

www.ingramcontent.com/pod-product-compliance
Lightning Source LLC
Chambersburg PA
CBHW050523170426
43201CB00013B/2060